Katharine

Katharine

A BIOGRAPHY OF HER ROYAL HIGHNESS THE DUCHESS OF KENT

Valerie Garner

WEIDENFELD & NICOLSON
LONDON

First published in Great Britain in 1991 by
George Weidenfeld & Nicolson Limited,
91 Clapham High Street, London SW4 7TA

British Library Cataloguing in Publication Data
Garner, Valerie
Katharine: Duchess of Kent
1. Great Britain. Kent, George, Duke of, 1902–1942.
Marina, Princess, Duchess of Kent, 1906–1968
I. Title
941.085092

ISBN 0-297-81175-4

Printed and bound in Great Britain by
Butler & Tanner Ltd, Frome and London

This book is dedicated to the Samaritans, Age Concern, Cancer Appeal Macmillan Fund, Helen House Hospice for Children and all those caring organizations so close to the Duchess of Kent's heart.

THE WORSLEYS OF HOVINGHAM

Sir Robert Worsley Kt = Alice Tildesley
of the Booths in the parish of Worsley, Lancs. Acquired the Manor
of Hovingham in 1563

Robert Worsley m. Elizabeth Gerard

Thomas Worsley m. Catherine Keighley

Thomas Worsley m. Elizabeth Wood

Thomas Worsley m.1 Alice Holcroft
(d. 1664) m.2 Penelope Egerton

Thomas Worsley m. Mary Arthington
(1649-1715)

Thomas Worsley m.1 Mary Frankland
(1686-1750) Great granddaughter of Oliver Cromwell
  (d. 1722)
  m.2 Anne Robinson

Thomas Worsley m. Elizabeth Lister
(1711-1778) (d. 1809)
Built Hovingham Hall

Thomas Worsley Edward Rev. George Worsley m. Anne Cayley
(d. 1774) (d. 1830) Rector of Stonegrave (d. 1854)
  (d. 1815)

Sir William Worsley m. Sarah Philadelphia Cayley
1st Bart. (d. 1885)
(1792-1879)

Sir William Cayley Worsley m.1 Harriet Philadelphia Worsley Arthington m. Marianne Hely-Hutchinson
2nd Bart (d. 1893) (1830-1861) (d. 1893)
(1828-1897) m.2 Susan Elizabeth Phillips
  (d. 1933)

Sir William Henry Arthington Worsley m. Augusta Mary Chivers Bower
3rd Bart (d. 1913)
(1861-1936)

  Lucy Vaughan Morgan m. Sir John Brunner, Bt
  (d. 1941)

Sir William Arthington Worsley m. Joyce Morgan Brunner
4th Bart (1895-1979)
(1890-1973)

Sir William Marcus John Worsley
5th Bart m. Hon. Bridget Assheton George Oliver John Arthington Katharine Lucy Mary
(b. 1925) m. H.R.H. The Duke of Kent

William Ralph Worsley Sarah Marianne Giles Arthington Peter Marcus
(b. 1956) (b. 1958) (b. 1961) (b. 1963)

By kind permission of English Life Publications

CONTENTS

ILLUSTRATIONS

ACKNOWLEDGEMENTS

The charges of sycophancy and hagiography so dreaded by royal biographers become increasingly difficult to avoid when glowing praise from all sides makes objectivity elusive. Searching for the real person, clues have to be carefully amassed, despite the curtain of royal mystique so assiduously preserved by courtiers. It does not help when, like the Duchess of Kent, the royal is of a modest disposition and prefers to weave her magic far from the media hordes who accompany the younger royal women. There was the unspoken but unmistakable inference that she did not consider herself biographical material and did not wish to be.

This understated attitude, fortunately, was not the view of the many men and women who know her well, either as personal friends or through her charitable work. Their help has been invaluable even though some preferred it to be off the record. Among those I would like to thank are Simon Armson, Linda Marsh, Susan Butler, Marion Needham, Caroline Oliver and John Cavanagh.

Sir Marcus Worsley, the Duchess's elder brother, was both hospitable and helpful when I visited Hovingham Hall and members of the Kent Household at York House, St James's Palace, including former Private Secretary Sir Richard Buckley, filled in many important details. Several colleagues were generous with help and advice particularly Martyn Lewis whose two moving television documentaries about the Duchess inspired the book in the first place and my good friend Christopher Warwick who was, as always, a source of wise counsel and encouragement.

My thanks also to Audrey Whiting, James Whittaker and my agent Doreen Montgomery for their interest in the project.

Finally I should like to thank my husband for being unfailingly supportive during the research and gestation of the book and for good humouredly transporting manuscript and pictures to and from the Weald of Kent.

INTRODUCTION

The unmistakable silvery blonde hair rolled back from her face was dripping with water as the fragile children surrounding her in the jacuzzi delightedly splashed their royal visitor. As children do, they frolicked round her hanging on to the swim suit she had borrowed on this visit to the Helen House Hospice for Children.

Clearly the Duchess of Kent is the exception to diarist 'Chips' Channon's view that 'royalty casts a strange atmosphere' or as architect Sir Hugh Casson once put it: 'Royalty in close proximity charges the air and causes behaviour to go into a different gear.' She behaved with those children as she would have done with her own three when they were younger, or her small grandson today. And the youngsters responded to her in the same completely natural way.

But those close to the Duchess know the depth of emotional commitment she gives to visits such as these. 'She has this extraordinary magical quality which helps her communicate with people who have a limited time to live,' her lady-in-waiting Sarah Partridge told me. 'We find she has to recharge her batteries after giving so much.' This sensitive gift, fuelled by Katharine Kent's personal strength, gallantry and discipline, has emerged since she herself went through a time of intense grief; a desolate mid-life depressive crisis which ignited, perhaps subconsciously, a spark which has never diminished to benefit others by her own experience.

There does appear to be an aura about this royal Duchess which makes every place she walks into somehow brightened by her presence. 'It is as if there is a light upon her,' said television presenter Martyn Lewis, a man not given to over-sell. 'As if there is a spotlight following her around – she seems to shine,' observed Susan Butler of the Cancer Appeal Macmillan Fund; 'a smile shining ahead of her like a light', noted writer John Edwards. Three shrewd and perceptive observers all had the same overwhelming impression of the Duchess of Kent who, as Katharine Worsley, married Prince Edward, Duke of Kent, the Queen's first cousin, in York Minster on 8 June 1961.

Then she was an attractive, unassuming Yorkshire girl who carried out her new royal duties in an understated, conventional way. Thirty years later she has become a tireless, surprisingly tough fighter, for one so naturally gentle, against any form of suffering that comes within her orbit. Like the Princess Royal she believes in 'field work' on behalf of the charities that have her patronage. This, for the Duchess, can include something as practical as washing dishes for a pensioner or taking her share of the duty rota on the Samaritan's caring and confidential service.

It is because she has been through deep depression herself that the Duchess is able to comfort those in most need of it with sensitivity and understanding. Above all she does it with a total lack of the unease which often seems to afflict people when confronted with the starker facts of illness and approaching death. 'It cheers me', she said once, 'to see how tears and smiles so often walk side by side.' This warm and inspiring woman, now fifty-eight, has come to terms with her own unhappy years and regenerated them into a passionate interest in helping others in trouble. 'I feel privileged and humble. Drained sometimes. Completely drained because you give an awful lot. It is giving and giving, very happily giving,' she told Martyn Lewis when he made a television documentary for ITN about her work at Helen House.

Her own experience helped her to understand the work of the Samaritans, an organization originally founded to help the suicidal and depressed. From the outset the Duchess's involvement has been that of a working patron who has been through the twelve-week preparatory course with other trainee volunteers. At one time she did a regular three- or four-hour duty at a central London branch. It could be a sex problem, illness, marriage break-up, suicide, even murder. Or just a lonely person desperate to talk to an understanding listener. Among those who telephone are drug-users and the Duchess's long hours with the Samaritans must have been especially poignant when her youngest son Nicholas was found by police in St James's Park, a stone's throw from his home at York House, in the possession of drugs – to the understandable distress of his parents. Hopefully it proved to be an isolated incident which has not been repeated but it underlined how such modern problems can beset royalty and commoners alike.

The Duchess learnt at first hand the substance, not the shadow, of the Samaritans' work. All too often a royal patron simply does not have the time to delve deeper into a project which carries their name on the letterhead. But Katharine is determined not to be just a figurehead. Her own experience of suffering taught her the importance of people not hiding within themselves, each in their own trouble; but sharing and helping each other out of their private wilderness, whatever it might be.

PART ONE

1

A Silver Spoon

The old mansion had known many births while the Worsley family had lived at Hovingham Hall. There was no reason to suppose that the baby girl born in a snow storm that bitterly cold twenty-second day of February, 1933, would have a future of any special significance. Indeed, as the only daughter in a family of three sons, she would be welcomed and much-loved but there would be no inheritance of Hovingham's three thousand rolling acres, or any foreseeable fame, for the small bundle in the crib upstairs.

But her arrival, early in the morning, created an air of deep happiness inside the Hall – an atmosphere that would continue as she grew up and which she would remember all her life. 'It was a very caring background. I felt very much loved,' she was to say in later years. The Hall, and an earlier manor house it had replaced, had sheltered the Worsleys since 1563 and seemed, like all homes in which one family has lived for generations, to be renewed and vitalized by this latest birth within its mellowed stone walls.

In the drawing room, where Worsley ancestors looked down from the walls, the family gathered round the third baronet and Squire of Hovingham, Sir William Worsley, as he lifted his champagne glass: 'To my granddaughter – to her long and happy life,' he said.

Katharine Worsley, the future Duchess of Kent, was born into a world that had apparently changed little since Edwardian days. Around her in the great house there was space, comfort and the warmth of a large and united family.

But it was a lifestyle soon to be threatened by events beyond the grey-stoned village and the four million acres of Yorkshire the child grew up to love so much. 'Yorkshire is a thread running through her life,' commented her lady-in-waiting, Sarah Partridge, almost six decades later.

But in 1933 it was not envisaged that Kate, as she soon became known, would stray far from the wide county of valleys, rivers, fells, dales and heather moors. Marriage, perhaps, to a neigh-bouring landowner to unite two old families in the customary way. But marriage to a royal Duke, making this baby 'Her Royal Highness' would have been dismissed as fantasy by the practical Worsleys who are direct descendants of the Puritan Oliver Cromwell – England's first and last dictator.

Those of the family who gathered to await the birth of a fourth child to the heir Captain William Worsley and his wife Joyce were relieved that their joyous personal news had, for the moment, replaced the grimmer tidings from the outside world. In Europe, where a flu epidemic had raged that winter, there was also the first stirrings of a turbulence that would rumble into a world war at the end of the decade, as a former house painter and army corporal, Adolf Hitler, took over as Chancellor of Germany.

In London, amid growing national and economic unrest, 50,000 demonstrators protested about unemployment in Hyde Park. Later on in the year, 30,000 Jews from Stepney, in East London, demonstrated against the Oxford Union's decision that it would not, in any circumstances, fight for King and Country. This unpatriotic resolution was passed despite the news that the Nazi Party had already begun to round up large numbers of Jews and herd them into concentration camps. This dispatch from overseas would have been perused in *The Times* and *Yorkshire Post*, always to be found in the library at Hovingham. But it may not have received the same attentive interest, despite its serious implications, as the news that England had won the Ashes after a controversial MCC tour of Australia. Captain 'Willie', as he was known, had captained Yorkshire in 1928 and 1929 and would eventually become President of the MCC. In the Hall, as in most Yorkshire households, cricket was almost a religion.

Katharine's birth had coincided with a heavy fall of snow which transformed the countryside, isolating farms and cottages in the Derwent valley and making travel almost impossible. But the Hall and its village are a small kingdom on their own and Joyce Worsley had a houseful of willing helpers to welcome her daughter.

In the nurseries, at the far end of the house, the snow produced howls of pleasure from the baby's two elder brothers when they awoke. Marcus, seven, was away at prep school but to Oliver, six, and John, four, the news of their sister's arrival almost certainly took second place to keen anticipation of sport in the snow. They hoped for a pitched battle or two, followed at teatime, with a candle-lit cake for Oliver because it was his birthday too. A coincidence that grew more agreeable as brother and sister grew older and celebrated together as much as possible.

Before they were let loose in the snow that wintry morning, the boys were taken to visit their mother in her bedroom warmed by a glowing fire, where they were introduced to their new sister. In the way of small boys they would have gazed wide-eyed at the infant as their parents remarked on her vivid blue eyes and the wisps of fair hair which would become distinctly ash-blonde in later years. No premonition warned Joyce Worsley as she cuddled her daughter that this tiny descendant of Cromwell, after whom her brother Oliver was named, would grow up to marry into the Royal Family. When it happened both families thought it a romantic, if ironic, twist to the tales of Roundheads and Cavaliers.

Although immensely proud of the Cromwellian ancestry – through his great-granddaughter, Mary Frankland, who married into the family at the beginning of the eighteenth century – the Worsleys of later years have been solid, upright Yorkshire squires with no leanings towards the anarchical ideals of Puritanism. Their lives, until Katharine became a royal Duchess, were well outside the milieux of the court, although they were certainly not overawed by royalty.

5

Worsleys entered Parliament, became Lord Lieutenants of the county and Justices of the Peace. In those capacities they met members of the Royal Family when they visited Yorkshire or, like the late Princess Royal, daughter of George V and Queen Mary, lived in the county. The family served Yorkshire with distinction in other ways, as soldiers, businessmen and philanthropic landowners. The future Duchess of Kent's father not only captained the cricket team – the ultimate accolade in the county – he also entertained some of the greatest cricketers of his day when they played at Hovingham against the local team.

But none of them have been courtiers like an earlier Worsley who, despite his Cromwellian connection, became an important aide to two Hanoverian Kings, George II and George III. Thomas Worsley, known as 'The Builder', inherited the estate in 1750 and set about putting his own distinctive and elegant stamp on a new house he built on the site of the old. Another ancestor, Sir James Worsley, was Keeper of the Wardrobe to King Henry VIII and governor of the Isle of Wight.

Sir Marcus Worsley, the present baronet, has researched the history of his family which can be traced back to the eleventh century. Hovingham became their home at a glorious, swashbuckling time in English history when Elizabeth I had been on the throne for thirty years. The Worsleys continued to live in the old manor house for another 187 years until Thomas Worsley, the sixth of that name, succeeded to the estate at the age of thirty-nine. He was the great-great-grandson of Cromwell but this did not prove an obstacle to royal service because he was a widely-travelled, erudite man who had much to offer the courts of the two Georges.

Because of his great love of horses he had chosen, instead of going to university or studying law, to attend the Swiss Riding School at Geneva where he gained a reputation as one of the most talented riders in Europe.

When he returned to England he became equerry to George II and, like others at court, could not fail to have been impressed with the flowering of the great Georgian aptitude for building. The King, Queen Caroline and Horace Walpole were substantial patrons of all that was best in the architecture, painting, furniture-making and sculpture of their day.

William Kent, Michael Rysbrack and Sir James Thornhill were among those at the height of their creative powers and Thomas the Builder – as he came to be known in the annals of Hovingham – was greatly influenced by their work.

When his friend King George III succeeded his grandfather he made Thomas an MP and Surveyor-General of the Board of Works in charge of all the royal buildings. This, according to his present-day descendant, Sir Marcus, gave him the opportunity to study the architecture and furniture of the royal palaces more closely. It meant 'the resources to carry out his ideas for building a house for his own pleasure, unique in its design'.

As George III and his Surveyor-General were both so deeply interested in architecture – the King studied under Sir William Chambers – it would be unusual if Thomas did not discuss his plans for Hovingham Hall with his Sovereign. Or show him the design, based on the concept of the sixteenth-century Italian architect, Andrea Palladio, of a Roman town house in classical times. Certainly the King generously gave a fine sculpture which was placed in the hall. The painting by Nicholas Poussin of Cephalus and Aurora, now in the drawing room, may have been acquired about this time.

George III admired Poussin and added his work to the royal collection which had been greatly enhanced by a hoard of art treasures, amassed by his Consul in Venice, Joseph Smith.

While helping young aristocrats on the Grand Tour buy Venetian paintings to take home, this astute diplomat had built up a renowned collection, destined to grace the residences of future British Kings and Queens.

Arrivals of such exciting acquisitions must have made Thomas's job immensely interesting. He was responsible for the upkeep of the royal palaces and would have supervised any alterations, as he did when Buckingham House – purchased from the Duke of Buckingham for £6,000 – was improved into a more fitting home for the Royal Family and became, eventually, a palace.

Thomas engaged Robert Adam to design a more impressive exterior, the plans of which he kept at Hovingham. In fact, they were never used although Adam designed new floors and ceilings commissioned by the Surveyor-General. Thomas Worsley's experience of his royal job encouraged him to try his hand at designing a new home for his family on the site of the old Hovingham Hall. But his fortune was limited and he had to go slowly with the building work which began in 1752 and continued over the next decade.

Thomas was one of the great riders of his day and, because of his passion for horses, was dubbed 'a rider of the great horse and architect' by Horace Walpole. Worsley himself referred to his horses as '. . . my music and I thank God I have yet an hand and an ear for them'.

It is not surprising that with such a love of horses he conceived a most handsome and novel entrance way for his fine new house. Hovingham Hall can still be entered today through the old stables and riding school where Thomas trained his horses, watched by the ladies of the house from the gallery above.

Through this unusual entrance in June 1961, came most of the remaining crowned heads of Europe when the daughter of the house married into the British Royal Family. Echoing, perhaps, in modern parlance what the diarist Arthur Young noted in 1769: 'I should apprehend with some horses that it might hazard the necks of many a coachful if the ladies persisted in not walking this approach'.

When William and Joyce Worsley's four children were growing up, the Samson Hall which adjoins the Riding School – still with its hexagonal oak blocks especially for carriages – was dominated by Giambologna's large marble group of 'Samson and the Philistine', the statue presented to his Surveyor-General and friend by George III.

It had been acquired when Buckingham House was bought and had a royal history, as it had originally belonged to a Medici prince, believed to have presented it to the Duke of Lerma. Subsequent owners were Philip IV of Spain and Charles I of England who gave it to the then Duke of Buckingham. When

Katharine was young it was a statue around which she and her brothers played. It stayed at Hovingham until just before her wedding when it was sent to the Victoria and Albert Museum.

The four children grew up with a similar pattern of life to most youngsters born into the old county families. As a clan the Worsleys are a pastoral breed with the Hall and its estate forming the heart of their lives. Like a magnet it continues to draw them home frequently, however far from their roots life has taken them.

Today Hovingham is only a short drive from the increasingly sprawling city of York and the motorways which link it to each end of Britain. But the fumes and noise still seem far away and the village, with its great old house, church, family-owned inn and the cluster of cottages, might be set in an earlier, more peaceful century.

When the Duchess returns she finds it almost unchanged despite a shortage, these days, of staff. Her brother and his son – another William who is godfather to the Kents' first grandchild – are trying to keep it that way. Even the gardens are still as beautiful as in Joyce Worsley's day because the present Lady Worsley – Katharine's sister-in-law Bridget – is as keen and knowledgeable a gardener as her mother-in-law who created the present, more manageable gardens.

Music, the Duchess's joy which she shares with her husband, has been a consuming passion for generations of Worsleys. The annual Hovingham Music Festival first evolved when the present generation's grandfather, the third baronet, had the notion that the indoor riding school had ideal acoustics for an auditorium. The first concert in 1887 was not only a resounding success but during it he met music-loving Mary Chivers Bower, from Scarborough, with whom he fell in love. They married three months later after an impetuous courtship.

Their union was wonderfully happy and set the scene for those who came after them. Music and cricket were the third baronet's notable interests and he contributed fully to Yorkshire's participation in both.

The Hovingham Music Festival became one of the events of

9

the county year, along with the Hovingham cricket matches which brought great cricketers from all over the world to the immaculate pitch which has been played on continuously since the early part of the nineteenth century. On this, one of the earliest private grounds, an all-England Eleven challenged twenty-two local cricketers. This historic match, in 1858, resulted in one of the earliest cricket photographs. The pitch, which is directly below the main windows of the Hall, is now the village cricket ground.

William and Mary Worsley had two sons and three daughters of which the eldest, another William, became the father of a future royal Duchess. His wife, Joyce, was a daughter of the hard-working, public-spirited Brunner family from Zurich bringing vigorous, 'new-rich' blood to the solid, worthy Worsleys.

The late Princess Marina, Duchess of Kent, used to say to her children 'Breeding will out' and if her conviction was well-founded the lineage of Katharine Worsley, destined to be her daughter-in-law, is an interesting one.

On her mother's side the founder of the British branch of his family was John Brunner. He left his native Switzerland as a young man and settled in Georgian England, fathering a family that not only worked hard and became rich, but channelled their resources back into the service of their adopted country.

John became a teacher in Liverpool and, in the 1830s, married a girl from the Isle of Man. Their two sons worked as clerks in the city and the younger, John, married a Liverpool girl and eventually became one of the founders of a chemical firm. It later became one of the group of companies which grew into the giant Imperial Chemical Industries.

When the Duchess of Kent, his great-granddaughter and a keen Liverpool supporter, visited the city with her husband – who is Chairman of the Football Association – to comfort survivors and bereaved families of the Hillsborough football disaster, she went as the only royal with direct family links with Liverpool.

John Brunner used much of his newly-acquired wealth philanthropically to endow educational facilities. He built schools and gave Liverpool University chairs of economics, chemistry and other studies which he considered appropriate to the way in which his money had been made – in the chemical industry.

He was created a baronet in 1895 when his granddaughter Joyce, Katharine's mother, was born. She grew up in a parliamentary family and when her father fought the 1906 election as a Liberal candidate, she and her brother became involved in the hustings as fervently as their parents.

As Joyce grew to womanhood, wealthy in her own right through her grandfather's family trusts, she became seriously interested in the Liberal party and worked for it for some years in the early Twenties. Then she met Captain 'Willie' Worsley and he fell in love with the attractive, capable young woman with her intelligent, cheerful attitude to life.

They were married in the spring of 1925 in St Margaret's, the parish church of Westminster, by the Archbishop of York, who, as a Worsley family friend, was invited to conduct the ceremony. It was attended by two former Prime Ministers, most of the villagers of Hovingham and the cream of Yorkshire and London society.

The following spring Joyce had her first baby: Marcus, now the fifth baronet, followed by Oliver in 1927 and John in 1928 – the year his father was chosen to captain the Yorkshire cricket team. Their only daughter was born five years later.

Katharine was a fortunate baby, as she would be the first to agree, born 'with a silver spoon in her mouth' in one of the bleakest years of the Depression. Britain's mass unemployment had reached flash point with desperate street riots and hunger strikes. When Prince George, later Duke of Kent, who would have been her father-in-law had he lived, visited London's East End he was greeted with cries of 'We want bread'.

Although there was suffering and deprivation all over the country, in the Worsleys' small, protected world, there were still maids in crisp white aprons, a cook-housekeeper in the old-fashioned kitchen quarters, a butler and a nanny to preside over the nurseries. All of which was normal in most large houses and provided work, helping – however insignificantly – the Yorkshire unemployment figures. Nowadays it has changed somewhat. Lady

11

Worsley opens the door herself and brings visitors a tray of tea and biscuits from the new modern kitchen she and her husband have installed.

In 1933, beyond the peaceful Hovingham boundaries, the shadow cast by Adolf Hitler and his Nazi party had less impact on the British than the stir created by H.G. Wells's new book: *The Shape of Things to Come*.

In it he predicted that 'the Soviet experiment would become hidebound in dogma' and that there would be war between Germany and Poland by 1940. Man would create a world state and live in peace by 2059. But another of the author's pronouncements of that era did not find much favour with the monarch when it reached the royal ears. Wells criticized the court and described it as 'alien and uninspiring'. 'I may be uninspiring,' retorted George V, 'but I'll be damned if I'm an alien.'

Anxious to make his royal house as British as possible, the King, whose own ancestry was mainly teutonic, had changed his family's name from the previous German titles to the very British 'Windsor' during the First World War.

Without doubt he would have approved the sound, no-nonsense, old-English names chosen for the babe whose paternal lineage could be traced back a thousand years in Britain and who would, one day, marry the King's Kent grandson – as yet unborn. She was christened in daffodil-time, at the Saxon font of the small church at Hovingham, and given the names of Katharine Lucy Mary.

2

That Dazzling Pair

When Katharine was seven months old an event occurred that was significantly to affect her own destiny. As she played in the nursery at Hovingham under the watchful eyes of Nanny Mist, many miles away in London a society hostess held one of her fashionable luncheon parties.

Lady Emerald Cunard was a leader of the set that scintillated around the Prince of Wales and for years she had been on Queen Mary's 'blacklist' because she was considered an unsuitable friend for the heir to the throne. Later, after the abdication, she found herself 'blackballed' in society by the new Queen Consort of King George VI because of her championship of the former King Edward VIII and Mrs Simpson before he decided to give up the throne for love.

'That awful woman', said Queen Elizabeth, using the same words as she would henceforth refer to her banished sister-in-law, the Duchess of Windsor. With the new reign Lady Cunard was not invited to any important social occasions and hostesses found themselves telephoning her when the King and Queen had left the party so that she could come along. For despite all her faults – and there were many – Emerald was popular.

In 1933, with George V still on the throne, her friendship with his heir, coupled with her own extraordinary, magnetic personality, ensured that her position was unassailable in society. A colourful, bizarre figure, she was, in the opinion of photographer Cecil Beaton, 'brilliant and often profound in a worldly cynical way'. In his memoirs he mentions 'her sense of melting sympathy in the presence of beauty, poetry and the people she loves'. Amongst those Lady Cunard herself would almost certainly have included the Prince of Wales's younger brother Prince George to whom she introduced his future wife.

To Emerald Cunard's house one spring day, came the beautiful, twenty-seven-year-old Princess Marina of Greece with her smooth dark hair and the lopsided, enigmatic smile that men found so attractive. There she met over luncheon the youngest of the three bachelor princes, soon to be created Duke of Kent.

It was an obvious mutual attraction at that first meeting but it was not until the following year that they met again. Once more the attraction between them was tangible and enchanted both Marina and 'Georgie', as he was known to the Royal Family. 'That dazzling pair', as diarist 'Chips' Channon described them, has been much-quoted but it pertinently sums up the way they lit up a room when they were together.

The latest royal romance set London buzzing with gossip. Prince George had behind him a wayward youth and stories about his exploits, some of them decidedly unorthodox, rekindled once again that summer season of 1934. For George did not come from the staid, dignified mould of his father, King George. His appetite for love equalled that of his grandfather King Edward VII and some of his relationships had been questionable at the very least. 'He had drunk deeply from life', according to 'Chips' Channon who knew him well.

Noël Coward was one of Prince George's intimates and it was a measure of Marina's understanding – for it was unlikely to be naivety – that he became her close friend also and remained so all her life.

George had other lapses in his past which still worried the Royal Family. At one time he had been addicted to drugs and was only cured by the devotion and patience of his elder brother, the Prince of Wales. He insisted that 'Georgie' stay with him at Fort Belvedere, his country retreat, where they both 'sat out' the agonizing drying-out period followed by an equally traumatic time of deep depression and breakdown.

Now, with that crisis safely behind him, the Prince was in cracking form, undeniably attractive and colourful with a highly developed taste for the unusual and unexpected that Marina found exciting and stimulating. Queen Mary, who had long cherished hopes of an alliance between her goddaughter and one of her sons, was optimistic that the close relationship developing between 'Min' and 'Georgie' might be the prelude to marriage. She was even more encouraged when reports filtered back through her ladies-in-waiting that they were constantly together.

George took the Greek Princess wining, dining and theatre-going. Afterwards they danced night after night at the Embassy Club, a favourite royal haunt, where the band played 'Love Is The Sweetest Thing' and 'I've Only Got Eyes For You' – the hit tunes of the time.

Soon Prince George had decided she was 'the only woman with whom I would be happy to spend the rest of my life'. And so it turned out, although, tragically, it was to be only a short life together.

Later that summer, staying with Marina's brother-in-law and sister Prince and Princess Paul of Yugoslavia, Prince George proposed and was accepted.

Prince Christopher of Greece was one of the family party staying in the shooting lodge in the Julian Alps. According to James Wentworth Day in *Princess Marina, Duchess of Kent*, he described later how '... everyone retired tactfully to bed until George and Marina were left sitting alone at opposite ends of the sofa. I had been in my bedroom about half an hour when I discovered I had left my cigarette case on the backgammon table. Putting on my dressing gown I went in search of it. The door to the drawing room was open; George and Marina were still sitting on the sofa, though no longer, I observed with satisfaction, at the opposite ends of it. I stole back to bed without my case.'

Both families were delighted. 'Marina is charming ... she will be a great help to my son,' a relieved Queen Mary commented to her lady-in-waiting, Lady Airlie. Shrewd and not unworldly, the Queen appreciated that it would take an exceptional woman to hold 'Georgie's' interest. Because she had been a princess in exile and lived and worked in Paris, Marina was thoroughly cosmopolitan. She had posed as a photographer's model and known freedom such as most royal princesses could only dream about: the joy of Paris in the spring, uncluttered by bodyguards or equerries; riding in the metro or eating in tiny bistros with a man friend. Like many young women she took such things for granted unlike her future descendants, forever on guard for 'paparazzi' cameras. Marina also worked in a home for Russian emigré children, helping to teach and care for them and, although her own family did not know extreme poverty, she was deeply aware of the suffering of other exiles in Paris.

At a time when the monarch's sons were still expected to marry women from similar backgrounds, Marina was a most unusual royal princess with an exceptionally distinguished pedigree. Her mother, Princess Nicholas, had been the Grand Duchess Helen Vladimirovna, granddaughter of Tsar Alexander II, niece of Tsar Alexander III and first cousin of the last Tsar, Nicholas II, murdered with the rest of his immediate family by the revolutionaries. Marina's father was Prince Nicholas of Greece, third son of King George and Queen Olga.

This background and her own innate sophistication and undeniable charm helped to make her marriage to Prince George so successful and, because of her royal ancestry, so acceptable to the King and Queen. Although they had warmly welcomed 'Bertie's' choice of an Earl's daughter, Lady Elizabeth Bowes Lyon, into the family eight years before, an alliance with another Royal House was customary practice amongst the kindred European royal families. In addition any children born to George and Marina would have royal blood on both sides of the family, a circumstance that Queen Mary, always preoccupied with lineage, fully approved.

As an additional bonus Marina's beauty was of a kind rarely seen in Britain, certainly not in the Royal Family – who tended to take after their Hanoverian forbears. Cecil Beaton, with his artist's eye, described her 'cool, classical features in a perfect oval head held high on a straight column of neck, the topaz eyes, the slightly tilted smile, the apricot complexion and the nut-brown cap of flat, silken curls'.

'Willie' and Joyce Worsley could not have missed the announcement of the royal engagement, although no glimpse into the future showed them the place their toddler daughter would occupy in the Kent family dynasty.

The royal wedding caught the public imagination and women everywhere were interested in the romance of such a glamorous couple. Marina struck exactly the right note when she asked everyone to share her happiness. 'As you know my years of exile have taught me how much unhappiness there is in the world ... I should be more than happy for the unemployed, and particularly their children, to receive any money which has been intended for the purchase of wedding gifts.'

The ceremony, on 29 November 1934, was the first royal wedding to be broadcast and it would almost certainly have been listened to at Hovingham because the Archbishop of Canterbury, as Archbishop of York, had married Katharine's parents.

'Never in history has a marriage been attended by so vast a company,' he said over the air. 'The whole nation are wedding guests.'

Prince George had chosen his elder brother as best man but for the Prince of Wales the day was not entirely happy. The brothers had been so close all their lives and now David felt lonely and curiously bereft. Wallis Simpson, soon to be his wife, was already perceptive enough to realize how he was feeling and shrewd enough, some say, to take advantage of the situation. In *The Heart Has Its Reasons* she wrote that, as she watched the Prince of Wales during the weeks preceding the wedding, 'it seemed to me that a sadness began to envelop him. He and his younger brother were very close and the bonds of blood were strengthened by an unusual kinship of spirit ... the gap in the Prince's life caused by his brother's marriage was not easily filled ... he was reaching out for something that was as yet unknown to him, something to which he could anchor his personal life.'

An appalled Royal Family and the nation learnt, in the course of the next few years, to which mainstay King Edward VIII, as he had become, planned to anchor his future life.

Unaware of their unwitting part in the future abdication drama, George and Marina were wed in Westminster Abbey on a typically misty November day. Marina was married from her godmother, Queen Mary's home, Buckingham Palace, and drove to her wedding in royal style in a semi-state landau accompanied by a Captain's Escort of the Life Guards. In a dress of silvery brocade woven with a design of English roses, by Edward Molyneux, Marina looked utterly beautiful. Diamond earrings, a matching necklace and small brooch enhanced the silver and white shimmer of the brocade and her veil of white tulle was secured by an impressive diamond tiara presented by the City of London. On her left shoulder was an oval miniature of George V surrounded by diamonds – the private order of the Royal Family which her new father-in-law had given her before the wedding.

As she walked slowly down the nave with her father, Prince Nicholas, Marina was followed by her eight bridesmaids, among them the small figure of the bridegroom's niece, Princess Elizabeth, destined to be Queen Elizabeth II. At eight years old she was deeply impressed by this dazzling new aunt whom the family called 'Min' or 'Mara'.

The public were even more enchanted by the new royal Duchess. 'They expected a dowdy princess – such as unfortunately my family are,' remarked the newly created Duke of Kent somewhat ungallantly, 'but when they saw this lovely chic creature they could hardly believe it.'

Marina swiftly established herself as a leader of fashion – much as the Princess of Wales is today. 'Marina Blue', her husband's favourite colour which she wore frequently, was all the rage; women bought cheap 2/6d copies of 'Marina' pill box hats with tiny veils and barmen named cocktails after the ravishing Duchess of Kent.

King George and Queen Mary showered their new daughter-in-law with costly jewellery – some of which Katharine, the present Duchess, inherited. From the King she received a *rivière* of thirty-six fine diamonds; from her mother-in-law, a sapphire and diamond tiara to match her engagement ring. Queen Mary also dipped into her own extensive collection to provide Marina – whose own family had sold most of their valuables during their exile, although some of the Romanov jewellery eventually came to the Duchess of Kent – with jewellery befitting a British princess.

They had an idyllic, five months honeymoon ending up in the West Indies, where they had their first meeting with President Roosevelt, who would become a close personal friend and god-father to their youngest child Prince Michael.

They returned to Britain to settle into their new home, number three, Belgrave Square, which Queen Mary had had redecorated for them whilst they had been away. By then Marina was expecting her first baby which diverted George to such an extent that he failed to notice how close his brother David and the now divorced Wallis Simpson had grown.

His Royal Highness Prince Edward, now Duke of Kent and Katharine's husband, was born early in the morning of 9 October 1935. His father remained with his mother throughout – the first royal husband to do so since Prince Albert with Queen Victoria. He did leave Marina briefly to talk to journalists who had been invited to wait in a ground floor room. 'I just thought I'd tell you that some hot coffee is being sent into you. After that I'm afraid the kitchens will be closed, but there'll be someone on duty just after six who'll get you some breakfast,' said the Duke.

It was a kindly gesture from the worried father-to-be who admitted: 'I do hope it will be over soon. I don't think I could stand much more of this.'

The birth of a royal prince who was, at that time, fifth in line to the throne, was greeted with some ceremony. A forty-one gun salute was fired by the Royal Artillery in Hyde Park and the Honourable Artillery Company fired a further salute from the Tower of London.

In Prince Edward George Nicholas Paul Patrick, the combined ancestry of his mother and father produced an infant who was very royal indeed. He is descended, through Empress Catherine of Russia and Queen Victoria, from the royal families of Romanov and Hanover, Saxe-Coburg-Gotha, Mecklenburg-Strelitz, Denmark, Greece and Britain.

King George V lived long enough to celebrate the birth of his new grandson, the first prince of the new generation. He recorded in his diary that Christmas at Sandringham: 'Saw my Kent grandson in his bath.' But a month later he died, leaving the throne, with deep misgiving, to his eldest son now Edward VIII. 'After I am dead the boy will ruin himself in twelve months,' he said shortly before retiring to bed at Sandringham for the last time. The kingly prophecy proved all too accurate.

In the 'Year Of The Three Kings', as 1936 came to be called, the BBC broadcast its first television programme at a time when the average family needed £6 a week to keep it above the poverty level. At Hovingham, the Worsley family mourned Katharine's grandfather, the third baronet, who died aged seventy-five. In London a scandal erupted which, however much the Royal Family might have wished it, would not go away.

For a time British newspapers remained silent about the new King's love for American divorcee, Wallis Simpson, although the foreign press blazoned it across the world. As the affair gathered momentum and developed into a crisis of deep significance to the future of the monarchy, it became impossible to maintain the discretion of the British media.

The Duke of Kent, the only one of the family close enough to David to have a chance of saving the situation, had to leave his pregnant Duchess and spend long days at Fort Belvedere trying to persuade Edward VIII to reconsider his decision to marry Mrs Simpson. 'He is besotted by the woman . . . one can't get a word of sense out of him,' despaired George. Although the brothers were so attached to one another – at one time they had shared York House, St James's Palace, where the Duke and Duchess of Kent live today – nothing George said could sway the King's resolve.

More than ever he was adamant that he would marry the woman he loved and, if necessary, renounce the throne. The Duke of York was next in line but for several days in December, 1936, there was an uneasy silence between the brothers. Two eminent royal biographers have put forward an intriguing theory to account for this. Denis Judd in his book *King George VI* wrote: 'It seems that in the highest circles there may have been some doubt as to whether the Duke of York would make an adequate monarch ... It is possible that serious consideration was given to the possibility of by-passing the Duke of York and offering the crown to his apparently more able and eligible brother, the Duke of Kent.'

At the time those close to the Prime Minister, Stanley Baldwin, also believed he had seriously considered the Duke of Kent as King. Not only was he a more impressive candidate than the stammering and diffident 'Bertie' but he already had a male heir – and his wife was royal in her own right.

Dermot Morrah who wrote two books 'with royal approval', one in 1947 – the year of Princess Elizabeth's wedding – wrote: 'It was certainly seriously considered at this time whether, by agreement among the Royal Family, the crown might not be settled on the Duke of Kent, the only one of the abdicating King's brothers who, at that time, had a son to become Prince of Wales and so avoid laying so heavy a future burden upon the shoulders of any woman.'

It is unlikely, however, in retrospect, that this suggestion would have been found acceptable. Glamorous and popular as the Duke and Duchess of Kent undoubtedly were, his history of drug addiction and sexual adventuring would have been a formidable handicap to what would have amounted to an arbitrary switch of dynastic rights.

But it poses the interesting conjecture that the present Duke of Kent might have been Britain's King and Katharine his Queen. But would he then have married the daughter of a Yorkshire squire? It is unlikely that they would have even met if, instead of being Duke of Kent, Edward had been Prince of Wales.

As it was the two children who would one day share their lives were brought up in very different backgrounds, although Kate was no stranger to beautiful furniture and classical surroundings, as Thomas the Builder had ensured when he built Hovingham for his family of the future. But its peaceful Arcadian setting was not a hub of power and social prestige as in a royal household. However simply the Kent children were brought up, their late grandfather had been King-Emperor and court protocol was taught to them even in nursery days. The nearest Katharine got to royal circles in London was when she visited the metropolis briefly on the way to spend summer holidays with her Brunner cousins on the south coast.

In those early years her happiest times were when her brothers came home from boarding school. Like Eddie Kent, who was some years younger, they went to Ludgrove Preparatory School and then Eton, but not at the same time as the Prince.

Although, in term time, she was virtually an 'only child', Kate was far from lonely. As the baby of the family, the chubby youngster with the distinctive flaxen hair was adored by her parents and the staff. She would have come close to being spoilt had it not been for the sensible views of her mother.

Joyce, although a Londoner born and bred, had settled down happily as the chatelaine of Hovingham Hall when her husband inherited the baronetcy. She particularly loved the gardens and her talented and dedicated work in them can be seen today, carried on by her daughter-in-law Bridget.

As a child Katharine followed her mother about the several individual flower gardens protected by high stone walls, wielding a miniature watering can in the wide, colourful herbaceous borders which, in summer, are one of the sights of Hovingham. She has loved gardening ever since and finds it 'immensely therapeutic'.

She had always had a special bond with her father. He entertained her with his jokes, imparted his knowledge of the countryside and was so patient, she now realizes, looking back, in answering her childish questions. The link between them grew as she progressed through childhood to leggy adolescence. They formed an easy, companionable relationship broken only by his death in 1973 when Kate was forty. 'My father even taught me to play cricket', the Duchess once told members of the MCC, reminding them proudly that he had not only captained Yorkshire but had been President of the MCC.

The Christmas of 1936, just before Kate's third birthday, was the usual happy reunion as her family gathered together in their home, with no special event marking it as out of the ordinary. But in Belgrave Square, that sunlit winter morning of 25 December, as a street musician played carols to assembled pressmen, the Duchess of Kent gave birth to a daughter. She was a sister for Prince Edward, named Alexandra after her great-grandmother, the late Queen Consort to King Edward VII. 'The nicest thing to have happened all year,' observed a delighted Queen Mary recovering from the trauma of the abdication at Sandringham.

The latest Kent baby grew up to be a staunch friend and affectionate sister-in-law to Katharine and a loyal, hard-working member of the Royal Family, fulfilling all the promise of her Christmas birthday.

3

A Village at War

Awartime childhood left many young emerging personalities
scarred in later life by a legacy of separation, injury, brutality
and the nightmare of bereavement. Compared to other children
all over the world who suffered as conflict tore their countries
apart, Katharine Worsley was more fortunate.

When war came to peaceful Hovingham village she was six
and a half, just old enough to remember Mr Day, the newly-
appointed air raid warden, coming to the Hall to fit everyone
with gas masks which were stored in the ballroom. As the Prime
Minister Neville Chamberlain announced the outbreak of hos-
tilities, the Worsley family, along with most of the villagers, were
in the small church attending morning service. There Kate and
her brothers had been christened and the inhabitants of
Hovingham have worshipped since Saxon times.

For the youngest Worsley the war did not mean leaving home
and loved ones like the sixty young evacuees from Durham who
arrived clutching their gas masks and with a tooth-brush, comb,
handkerchief and set of spare clothing each. Some had never been
in the country before. 'He hadn't even seen a cow or sheep,'
said Kate in astonishment about a boy she had met at Sunday
School.

Sir William went off to join his regiment 'The Green Howards'
and Lady Worsley was left to run their home and the estate in
his absence. The household had one more member, however,

24

Miss Evelyn Brockhurst who, because she was past calling-up age, took the job as Katharine's governess.

Soldiers, who camped in the grounds, surrounded the Hall and Kate could no longer wander freely or ride her pony through some of the woods. They were 'out of bounds' until her brothers came home from boarding school and she could go further afield with them. The soldiers were allowed to play cricket on the famous Hovingham pitch and Kate learnt how to collect any shrapnel that had fallen on the green lawns. Sometimes, she joined in a game, using the light, miniature cricket bat her father had given her when he showed her how to use it.

She learnt to sew also, as women and children were doing all over Britain, fired by the example of Queen Elizabeth who held sewing parties in the Balcony Room at Buckingham Palace. Lady Worsley, always a keen Women's Institute member, asked local women to join her in the Tapestry Hall at Hovingham. They worked beneath walls hung with ancient tapestries and flanked by classical and Renaissance sculptures, sitting at a massive table made of two huge planks of elm which was originally downstairs in the servants' hall.

Around them were five sets of armour which, three centuries before, had been held by the Lords of the Manor to equip men of the village when they were called to the colours.

Soon Katharine was joined by a cousin, Diana Colgate, and her companionship made the summer of 1940 a happy one for the two young girls, unaware as they were of the Battle of Britain beginning to be waged in the skies or the disaster of Dunkirk. They were tense days when everyone except the smallest children gathered round the wireless set at news time. Kate was too young to notice how her mother's face tightened with strain if the news was bad, although as she grew older and more sensitive, it was the barometer which indicated whether she needed cheering up by her young daughter.

In the Cotswolds the Duke and Duchess of Beaufort were hosts to some very important evacuees. At the outbreak of war, Queen Mary had gathered up two of her grandchildren, Edward and Alexandra of Kent, and taken them to the comparative safety of

Badminton House. She arrived with seventy pieces of luggage, an entourage of sixty-three men and women and her two grand-children. They were all transported in twenty cars – 'Quite a fleet', noted her daughter-in-law, the Queen, as they set off from Sandringham.

Installed at Badminton, Queen Mary took up her self-delegated war work of ivy-clearing and the Kent children were expected to help along with the evacuees from Birmingham. Most of them did not realize that the tall, stately lady with the long stick which she brandished freely was Queen Mary, mother of the King. She had declared immediate war on one of her pet hates, the ivy clambering over trees on the vast estate and older members of the Royal Family would have been amused if they could have been there to see her in action. The Queen had always been formidable with a walking stick, or even a parasol, with which she used to prod her husband King George V when he swore – which was frequently. Often Queen Mary, Eddie and Alex and any member of her ivy-clearing party who could find a space could be seen riding through the estate in a horse-drawn farm cart. It was requisitioned by HM whenever she spotted ivy that needed clearing in a distant corner of the grounds. More used to travelling by limousine or royal landau, she was delighted to be saving petrol. 'Aunt May, you look as if you are in a tumbril,' said the Duchess of Beaufort, eyes twinkling. 'Well, it may come to that yet, one never knows,' said Queen Mary.

Later she turned her attention to salvaging anything found lying about the grounds – old tin cans, bottles and scrap of all kinds were gathered up and sent off for recycling to help the war effort ... But sometimes the Queen Dowager was over-enthusiastic which, as her friend Sir Osbert Sitwell recalled, could lead to misunderstanding. Queen Mary found 'a large piece of rusty iron. She dragged it, personally, to her dump but a short time later, a local farmer arrived in great consternation. The Queen was informed: "Please Your Majesty, a Mr Hodge has arrived and he says Your Majesty has taken his plough and will Your Majesty graciously give it back to him, please, at once, as he can't get on without it!"'

When they relaxed from their labours, Queen Mary taught her lively and mischievous Kent grandchildren some of the ways of the court and the 'ancien regime' that was their heritage. Alexandra, nearly four, learnt to curtsey – sweeping her grandmother a deep and perfect court curtsey, the art of which has never left her; Eddie, rising five, was taught to bow and kiss his grandmother's hand. At the old Queen's knee they learnt to read, or listened as she told them stories about their ancestors. The irony of it was that, as Queen Consort, she had not had the time or inclination to do the same for her own children, who never had the same close relationship with their parents. Queen Mary drilled into the sometimes unruly and impetuous pair that they were royal children and they must always remember it in the future. Years later Princess Alexandra was asked how she managed to stand so long without tiring. 'You must remember', she replied, 'that I was trained to do so by my grandmother, Queen Mary.'

The children's mother, Marina, was working incognito as a voluntary auxiliary nurse at University College Hospital. She was known as Nurse Kay and did all the routine work of a ward, including surgical dressings, bedmaking, washing patients, feeding and handing round meals. She nursed bomb victims, never bothering to go to the shelter herself when the sirens went – the ward was just too busy. One day her husband, Prince George, visited the hospital in an official capacity. Marina was presented to him with a group of nurses and solemnly gave him a curtsey. Then she quietly followed him round the ward, walking well back from his escort of hospital officials ... One day one of the doctors remarked: 'One of the VADs in No 16 looks the spitting image of the Duchess of Kent.' Then he forgot all about it, but one of the patients was not fooled so easily. She worked for a dressmaker and had seen pictures of the fashionable Duchess in a magazine. 'I've seen her picture dozens of times,' she said. 'Nobody is going to tell me it isn't her.'

His wartime job inspecting RAF bases meant that the Duke of Kent was often able to visit his mother and the children when he was in the West Country. Both he and Queen Mary shared a passion for old furniture and he used to take her 'antiquing' in and around Bath. 'To Queen Mary his visits to Badminton were a source of sparkling joy,' wrote her biographer James Pope-Hennessy.

Although they were considered safe at Badminton it turned out to be as vulnerable as any country district in the south of England, although Queen Mary – once thoroughly settled in – stayed there throughout the war and was quite sad to leave at the end of it. But one day a tangible reminder of the danger facing London and other big cities arrived in the shape of unexploded bombs in the vegetable garden which caused great excitement when they were exploded by a bomb disposal crew.

At Hovingham the war proceeded rather more quietly but when Kate's brothers came home for the holidays they showed her the searchlights she had not noticed before, hidden as they were behind the blackout curtains. The boys, more knowledgeable about such things than their sister, explained how they caught the enemy bombers in their sweeps so that the gunners in their anti-aircraft sites outside York could see them.

Marcus, Oliver and John lost no time in meeting all the new faces on the estate and in the village and their small sister trailed after them on their expeditions – sometimes on their ponies but often by bicycle. Landgirls had replaced the men and there were searchlight crews as well as soldiers in the grounds.

At harvest time everyone lent a hand and Kate and her brothers learnt the backbreaking jobs the landgirls now did so effortlessly. In the kitchen she helped with the jam-making – a job she still likes to do in her own home today with fruit she has picked herself from the Queen's gardens at Sandringham.

Lady Worsley had by now thoroughly involved herself in Yorkshire affairs. She worked for the county WVS (Women's Voluntary Service), was President of the local Women's Institute, Founder and President of a children's home in York and organizer of a parish produce association for the marketing of home-grown produce.

Under her mother's able tutorage Kate learnt to live up to the

Worsley creed of helping others which, as an apprenticeship for royal service, could not have been bettered.

A very genuine desire to become, as her mother put it, 'a good person' was kindled in the ash-blonde, slightly tubby youngster who was, even then, a small, sparkling presence in her own right. 'I remember she was always very strong,' said her eldest brother. By that he did not mean bossy, but strong-willed and fearless – a characteristic that was to be tested in future years.

In 1942 when Katharine was nine and her future husband, Eddie Kent, almost seven, his father was killed in a tragic and incomprehensible flying accident just a few weeks after the birth of his youngest son, Prince Michael. The Duke, as an Air Vice Marshal in the RAF, was flying to Iceland in a Sunderland flying boat when the accident occurred.

Despite an experienced, hand-picked crew led by Flight Lieutenant Frank Goyen with one thousand operational hours behind him, the aircraft inexplicably crashed on a heather-clad Caithness hillside, killing all but one on board. He was Sergeant Andrew Jack, the rear gunner, whose turret was thrown clear of the wreckage. He fought his way into the burning plane and carried out fellow crew members, among them the Duke of Kent.

At Balmoral the King and Queen were dining with the Duke and Duchess of Gloucester when the news came; Queen Mary was at Badminton when the telephone rang and the King told his mother of her youngest – and favourite – son 'Georgie's' death. Her first thought was for her daughter-in-law and the children who had adored their father. 'I must go to Marina tomorrow,' said the indomitable Queen Dowager.

Marina, whose youngest child was only seven weeks old, was tired and had gone to bed early. When her old nurse Kate Fox (Foxy) gently broke the news she collapsed and was still in a state of shock, alternately weeping or staring into space, when Queen Mary arrived next day.

Her close friend Baroness Agnes de Stoeckl (Auntie Ag to the children) remembered the happiness of their last day together at Coppins. 'Perfect sunshine ... the ducks quacked, the turkeys laughed, the cocks crowed ... the whole of Coppins seemed a mass of flowers . . .' As he left his wife and family for the last time the Duke, handsome in his RAF uniform, spoke words that, in retrospect, seem curiously prophetic. Patting his pet chow he said: 'What will you do with him when I am gone?'

News of the Duke's death on active service saddened the Worsleys. He had visited them in 1939 after engagements in York, to open a new village hall. His photograph still hung there – the only royal picture in a village which has several of Cromwell. Kate was briefly introduced to the father-in-law she would never know and he picked her up and swung her high in his arms as he did with his own children.

For Edward, then only six, the loss of his father, whom he so much resembles, went deep. In the short time they had together they had established a closer, loving bond than was usual, at that time, between royal fathers and sons. Agnes de Stoeckl wrote in her diary how George each evening 'carries his son to the nursery and lays him in his cot and stands watching and waiting. Nanny told me that each night as he lays his son in his cot she discreetly leaves the room but she can hear the Duke talking softly to him.'

It was apparent, as the boy grew older, that he had also inherited his father's talent for anything mechanical. Writer Audrey Whiting mentions that 'at four, lovingly watched by George, he could take a toy motor car to pieces and quickly reassemble it'.

Explaining to her elder children that their father would not be coming home was the most difficult task of Marina's life and it fell to Queen Mary, who knew her Kent grandchildren so well, to enlarge on her daughter-in-law's brief, tearful words and talk gently to Eddie and Alex about their father.

In the September of 1943, as allied troops invaded the toe of Italy, Kate began school. She was ten years old and only 'a droopy day', as non-boarders were called at St Margaret's School. But Kate lived so close to Castle Howard, home of their friends and neighbours, the Howard family, where the school was based, and Lady Worsley wanted to keep her youngest at home as long as possible. Her brother Marcus remembers she used to ride to school on her pony 'Greylegs'. She cut a small figure with her warm red school cloak flying behind and her blonde hair in two pigtails, on her way through the woods to the historic mansion which Horace Walpole described as 'a palace, a town, a fortified city'. It had, he wrote after a visit, 'temples on high places, woods worthy of being each a metropolis of the druids, vales connected to hills by other woods, the noblest lawn in the world fenced by half the horizon and a mausoleum that would tempt one to be buried alive. In short I have seen gigantic places but never a sublimer one.'

Television viewers know Castle Howard as the setting for *Brideshead Revisited* by Evelyn Waugh and to all this magnificence Katharine went each day, arriving in jodhpurs with her gas mask slung round her shoulders.

Being a day girl she missed sleeping in the dormitory considered the best by the boarders, once Lady Georgina Howard's sumptuous yellow and gold bedroom. It was still very luxurious except that the spartan belongings of the girls had taken the place of extravagant draperies and the elegant bed. Not unnaturally Kate, like most day girls, felt a bit out of things and was torn between the wish to go home to familiar surroundings and staying to enjoy the fun the boarders seemed to enjoy. She was inclined to be sensitive about being 'only a day girl' and liked the mornings she rode her pony to school because running round from the stables was less conspicuous than arriving by car.

Her good-natured, easy charm was already evident. 'A delightful child to have in the class,' noted her form mistress. 'Very merry and bright and ready for a bit of mischief.' Kate did not like Latin but was good at most other subjects. 'She thoroughly enjoyed games and gymnastics and was good at them and particularly good at cricket.' Music was always her special subject. 'Very musical and artistic generally', said one report.

Like wartime schoolchildren in country districts all over Britain, the girls of St Margaret's helped in the fields, particularly at potato picking time. At Castle Howard some of the workers were Italian prisoners with whom Kate was especially popular because of her blonde hair and fair colouring. She even learnt a smattering of Italian, including affectionate, admiring endearments like 'Cara Bellissima' from men who were missing their own young families.

In the spring of 1944 as daffodils cast their golden carpet over the slopes and dells of the estate and along the banks of the Derwent, the King and Queen made a top-secret visit to Castle Howard. They were visiting troops preparing for the invasion of Europe. In Winston Churchill's words: 'The hour of our greatest effort is approaching.' Among the servicemen camped in the grounds of great Yorkshire houses like Castle Howard and Hovingham Hall, there was a tense feeling of expectancy and a brittle cheeriness which masked the inevitable anxiety of men about to go into battle.

The school was told of the visit shortly before the royal party arrived and lined the imposing drive leading down from the obelisk, their red school cloaks above blue skirts and white blouses making an appropriate splash of patriotic colour.

With the King and Queen was Princess Elizabeth who would soon be joining the ATS (Auxiliary Territorial Service) and Kate had her first glimpse of the two royal women who, seventeen years later, would become her 'Aunt Elizabeth' and 'cousin Lilibet'.

Within three months came D-Day with the first allied troops landing in France. The following May, Kate's red cloak joined all the others in the school as part of the Victory-in-Europe decorations at Castle Howard. They ripped the sheets off the beds and added blue summer uniforms to the impromptu festive display decorating Vanbrugh's Palladian masterpiece. The third Earl of Carlisle, planner of Castle Howard in 1702, might have thought the improvised decorations inappropriate to the splendour of his mansion but would surely have approved their ingenuity in the face of wartime shortages.

Afterwards there was a giant bonfire with a sing-song round the flames for which day-girl Kate stayed on, nibbling charred potatoes – baked on the fire – in between joining in the chorus of 'forties' songs with her fine soprano voice.

In the more formal background of Buckingham Palace the Duchess of Kent and Eddie and Alexandra joined other members of the Royal Family on the balcony. Below them happy crowds cheered and sang the national anthem.

The following week the Kents again took part in a royal occasion – riding in the State procession for the National Service of Thanksgiving at St Paul's Cathedral in the City of London. Edward, still a shy prep schoolboy, dreaded the occasions when he felt everyone was looking at him and used to duck down below the level of car or landau window, from time to time, to get away from it all.

To further celebrate VE Day, the girls of St Margaret's were given a holiday and told they could cycle into York if they wished. With her friend Diana Hyne, Kate made her way to the noble medieval Minster where, on just such a day seventeen years later, she would wed a royal Duke with three Queens and most of the European royal families among the congregation.

The Minster holds a special meaning for Yorkshire folk and on VE Day many visited it, along with the schoolgirls from Castle Howard. Even as a young girl the great church held a spiritual significance for Kate although she may not have been wholly conscious of it then. Outside jubilant crowds noisily celebrated victory but inside the Minster there was a calm serenity which spanned the thirteen centuries it had stood there. It seemed to hush even the footsteps of those who paused within its walls on that day of national rejoicing.

In Badminton, Queen Mary surprised everyone by going to the local pub after dinner where the village was celebrating. She joined in all the songs, singing – as one of them said – 'in a loud, lusty voice' all the old favourites.

Lady Worsley had prepared a superb tea, using most of the household rations to bake an extra-special victory cake to welcome Kate and her friend when they arrived back at Hovingham – hot, tired and thirsty – after their day in York and the long cycle-ride home. Then they went back to school for the rest of the term but, at nearly thirteen, Kate would not be returning to St Margaret's in September.

The fear of invasion was over and her parents decided to send her to Runton Hill School near Norwich where her cousin had been so happy. At last she was a boarder and in a school which her mother later described as 'providing an education varied, humane and individual'.

It was also quite spartan and fuel rationing meant little or no heat with which to face the harsh Norfolk winters. The year of 1947, when Kate was fourteen, was the worst. It brought sub-zero temperatures and the coldest weather for years. In Norfolk the RAF had to drop supplies for stranded villages and Lady Worsley wrote that the same was happening in Yorkshire. Every-where the lack of fuel brought cuts in electricity. In London Buckingham Palace was candlelit as were government offices, the law courts and shops. Four million people lost work through power cuts, trains carrying coal were stranded in snow drifts and Sheffield was without milk. Isolated farms hung out sheets as distress signals to the RAF and one village in Devon sent a stark telegram on 12 February which read: 'No bread since 27 January. Starving.' It was all part of the harsh austerity which faced post-war Britain. Clothes and food were still rationed and morale was not improved by the Labour government's official slogans: 'Export or Die' and 'Work or Want'. In London over a thousand people queued for potatoes and the tinned meat ration was cut to twopence a week. Kate – or Kathy as some of her school friends called her – became as stoical about it as everyone else for few in post-war Britain could remember life with no shortages.

In the middle of it all, in war-torn Paris, Christian Dior laun-ched his 'new look' which a then junior trade minister called Harold Wilson condemned as 'irresponsibly frivolous and waste-ful', because it used yards of material. But it gave women an 'hour-glass' look and a much needed boost to their spirits. Somehow, everyone from Princess Elizabeth downwards managed to beg, borrow or scrounge the means to have at least one such dress and the girls at Runton Hill longed to do the same.

Later that year the wedding of Elizabeth and Philip Mountbatten – Marina's cousin – brought, as Churchill put it: 'a flash of colour on the harsh road we have to travel'. As cousins of both the bride and bridegroom, the Kent children played prominent parts in the ceremony: Alexandra as a bridesmaid and

Edward, still a twelve-year-old schoolboy, escorting his elegant mother, the Duchess. Katharine, like all schoolgirls, was enthralled with the romance of the young Princess and watched the film of the ceremony in the school's improvised cinema, unaware of what the future held. Her own wedding in 1961 would be very similar, echoing the colourful pageantry and ritual but in York Minster not Westminster Abbey, by her own choice.

At Heathfield, where Princess Alexandra was at school, it was decided that all the girls could go to the local cinema in Ascot to see the wedding film. Alexandra was horrified lest her part in the wedding would be construed as 'showing off'. She burst into tears and begged not to go. 'I'm in it – they'll see me,' she cried. 'Please don't make me go. It will be so awful . . . I can't bear it.'

Kate stayed at Runton Hill for a further two years. Although she was 'an exceptionally well integrated girl', she had no apparent leadership qualities and had never been Head Girl or Head of House.

She had, however, excelled at games, particularly lacrosse and captained the school's first team. As at St Margaret's music was her best subject and during her last year at school Kate was secretary of the music society. She organized visits to concerts and recitals and the experience helped her with a special project two years later – the revival of the Hovingham Music Festival inaugurated in 1887 by her grandfather.

Katharine left school to face the beginning of adult life but before she said goodbye to the spacious Edwardian house which had always seemed to be battered by cold winds from the North Sea, she demonstrated her growing musical talent by playing a movement of a Mozart concerto in the school concert.

4

The Two Ks

There was clearly no brilliant academic brain behind the clear blue eyes and well-chiselled features of 'the Worsley girl', as she was known in the county. Her brothers smiled tolerantly when told that she, too, was going up to Oxford. But it was in no ancient college that Kate, now seventeen, took up residence.

A pass in French oral and a merely respectable credit in English literature was all she could muster scholastically and it was not enough. Marcus, seven years older, took an honours degree in modern history at New College and had already left to join the BBC. But the two younger Worsley brothers were still at Trinity when their young sister was enrolled at Miss Hubler's Finishing School in Merton Street.

In the post-war world of Oxford in 1950, with veteran ex-servicemen and women undergraduates working and playing hard to catch up on the lost years, the girls at Miss Hubler's lived a curiously outdated existence. French literature, painting and history were taught by the Principal herself. Cookery lessons were taught by a French woman and Kate continued her music studies with a talented Austrian teacher.

The place was so exclusive, in fact, that there were less than a dozen pupils, all carefully watched over in the genteel way of good finishing schools at that time. Kate managed to escape as often as possible with her two brothers, Oliver, who read agriculture and John, history. Her seventeenth birthday was Oliver's twenty-third and they had a party with food brought in from the pub on the corner near Oliver's digs. It made a change from the government-sponsored 'British Restaurant' with its standard 1/3d lunch where brother and sister more usually met.

The Oxford year was one of transition from schooldays to adulthood and in completing her education Kate faced an inevitable decision about her future. The pull of music was strong and so was the love she had for children. But with no real plans she was in danger of drifting until a suitable marriage came along.

Her parents were comfortably off and provided a cushion against the realities of the difficult working world of post-war Britain where demobbed men and women were chasing too few jobs. Many girls in her position would have accepted the easy life, staying at home until something came up; instead Kate found herself a job at St Stephen's Children's Home in York. There she tended not only children in need of care and orphans, but took in her stride the more menial tasks around the Home.

She cleaned out fireplaces, washed floors, made beds, mended and cooked – whatever needed doing. Her hands grew red and sore during the winter of 1951 but she persevered, saying cheerfully: 'Someone has to do it.'

'She was always happy. There was nothing she wouldn't do. The children loved her singing about the place and she adored them,' said one of the staff. With Kate's fund of commonsense, inherited from her mother, combined with a considerable affinity towards children, it seemed clear that her vocation lay in the direction of child-care. The youngsters at St Stephen's felt the empathy she had for them and 'idolized her', according to a colleague. 'Kate always had time for them,' said the matron, Mrs Elsie Cobb, years later. She even spent one Christmas at the Home because she wanted to be with her young friends and often took sad little ones from broken homes back to Hovingham for the weekend. There they made for the old nurseries and raided the toy cupboards where Kate and her brothers had left their old favourites.

The month she became nineteen King George VI died, on 6 February 1952. His eldest daughter, now Elizabeth II, and her husband flew back from Kenya where they had cut short a Commonwealth Tour, to enter the dawn of a new reign.

Katharine Worsley now explaining to the children at St Stephen's that they had a new Queen would find herself playing an unexpected part in the Kent family team. She would become one of the close family members who form a loyal tightly-knit circle around the Queen. Earl Mountbatten mentioned the strong supportive role played by the Kent family when he explained to Audrey Whiting: 'To be a Monarch and have cousins like the Kents is of untold value. They are both relatives, friends and, at the same time, bloody hard-working people.'

As she faced her daunting future, the Queen declared: 'I shall always work, as my father did throughout his reign, to uphold constitutional government and to advance the happiness and prosperity of my peoples, spread as they are all the world over ... I pray that God will help me discharge worthily this heavy task that has been lain upon me so early in my life.'

As Lord Lieutenant of the North Riding of Yorkshire and the Queen's representative, Sir William decided regretfully that he must cancel a dance planned for Kate's birthday on the twenty-second. Instead she celebrated with the children of St Stephen's who loved her large birthday cake and helped her blow out nineteen candles in the dining room of the Home.

For the Duke of Kent, still a gangling, diffident sixteen-year-old, the death of his uncle meant the public ordeal – for one so shy – of walking with the Dukes of Edinburgh, Windsor and Gloucester in the funeral procession. He flew back from Le Rosay School in Switzerland, where he had gone after Eton, to be fitted with a long, sombre black coat and top hat – the only royal Duke not in uniform. The day before the funeral he and Alexandra were taken by their mother to see George VI Lying-in-State at Westminster Hall. They were escorted in through a side door from the House of Lords and stood quietly beside the coffin, which was draped with the Royal Standard they had last seen flying over Sandringham House when the family had gathered for the last time with 'Uncle Bertie' at Christmas. A year later Edward was again walking in a funeral cortège, that of his grandmother Queen Mary, with whom he had spent formative childhood years, who died on 24 March, at the age of eighty-five.

Later that year at the June Coronation of his first cousin 'Lilibet', seventeen-year-old Edward, in the robes of a royal Duke, his coronet held by a page, was third to kneel in homage to the new Sovereign – after her husband, the Duke of Edinburgh, and uncle, the Duke of Gloucester. He performed this obeisance perfectly, except that he forgot to remove his gloves before kneeling before the Queen.

For Edward, as for all the Queen's family, the Coronation was an emotive experience. As the crown of St Edward was placed on her head, the royal Dukes – except the former King who did not attend – placed coronets upon their own heads. Then, led by Philip, they knelt, one by one, to swear the historic oath: 'to become your liege man of life and limb and of earthly worship; and faith and truth I will bear unto you, to live and die, against all manner of folks. So help me God.' As the young Duke of Kent finished pledging his fealty, he rose, and climbed the steps of the throne, touched the crown with his hand and kissed his cousin's left cheek.

Taking part in the Coronation ritual left a deep impression on Eddie Kent. For the first time he was fully conscious of the ancient heritage of his family and of the duties and penalties such a birthright imposes.

Sir William, in his official capacity, was present in the Abbey with Lady Worsley and Katharine watched the ceremony on television at her brother John's flat. Already fate was drawing together the threads of their separate lives as the future Duchess of Kent, unaware of her destiny, watched the Duke kneel before the Queen.

With two brothers – Marcus and John – already living in London, she decided to follow her instincts and find a job there. After a year at St Stephen's she wanted to move on to more professional work with children.

Lady Patricia Eden, sister of Sir Anthony, was an old friend of the Worsleys and had started a school for girls and younger boys in Kensington. It was successfully established and she would not have jeopardized it by employing the daughter of friends if she was not up to the job. Kate had none of the usual training, such as Froebel or Montessori, but her experience at St Stephen's weighed heavily in her favour and she was employed as a kindergarten teacher at a salary of £12 a month.

'I remember she was always cheery and sparkling but one sensed a deep reserve beneath the surface,' said one of her colleagues. Kate was in charge of the youngest pupils with all the attendant chores small children require. In many ways it was St Stephen's over again – a regular nine-to-five existence with her twenty-first birthday just a routine working day, although the children sang her 'Happy Birthday'. But there was a lively party in the evening, organized by her brothers.

That same year John married Carolyn, daughter of Viscount Hardynge and Kate was asked to be a bridesmaid. Lord Hardynge had met his Canadian wife whilst serving as ADC to the Governor-General of Canada and had settled there, becoming a prominent and influential businessman. The wedding of their daughter to John Worsley was in Ottawa and Kate flew over with her family for her first visit to the country she grew to love so much.

Meanwhile the Duke of Kent had entered Sandhurst Military Academy as a cadet and was finding, as all bachelor princes do, that he inevitably attracted much media interest. As he grew uneasily resigned to this he found that it was not always accurate, often unkind and hardly ever went down well with his family. The Duke found himself described as 'Britain's most eligible man' – which he probably was at that time – although certainly not because of his money as he had to live on his army pay. 'The Playboy Prince' and the 'Speed-loving Duke' were other titles bestowed by gossip columns, all fairly mild by today's media standards, but they bred in Eddie the seeds of his dislike of personal publicity that is so apparent today.

Accounts of his various girlfriends were of more interest to the media than his steady progress through military college where he won the Sir James Moncrieff Grierson prize for foreign languages and also passed the French interpretership examination. He was eventually posted to the Royal Scots Greys and, as it

turned out, became the finest soldier the Royal Family has
produced, according to military circles. He served with his regiment at home and overseas, reaching the rank of Lieutenant
Colonel. The greatest disappointment of his army career was
when he was not allowed, for security reasons, to serve in Northern Ireland.

The Duke had always been destined for the army and never
wavered from his early decision, confirmed after watching his
widowed mother review the Royal West Kent regiment of which
she was Colonel-in-Chief. 'What a long time you have been,' said
the small boy who had missed most of the proceedings and
become bored. 'I have very little of my own, Eddie,' replied the
Duchess. 'But these are my men.'

Like another Prince Edward, as yet unborn, he might have
chosen a less conventional career had it been three decades later.
The background of the Kent family was always cosmopolitan
with theatrical overtones. Marina's aristocratic European friends
like Turia Campbell, before her marriage Princess Galitzine,
Baroness Agnes de Stoeckl who lived in a cottage on Coppins
estate and her daughter Zoia Poklewska-Koziel were constantly
around. They mixed easily with her show-business friends like
Noël Coward, Douglas Fairbanks, Cecil Beaton and Danny Kaye.
The small court at Coppins or in the London apartment at
Kensington Palace was sparkling and amusing; an effervescent
contrast to Marina's dignified, reserved life in public. At the time
he entered Sandhurst, the Duke of Kent was losing his earlier
shyness and, like most young men, he was gaining more confidence.

But he could be uncommunicative and reserved to the point
of curtness and had inherited the sudden outbursts of temper
which were a noticeable trait of male descendants of Queen
Victoria. Edward VII was particularly liable to flare up uncon-
trollably as was Eddie's 'Uncle Bertie'. But after his marriage,
the future George VI's irritability was usually quelled by an
understanding look from his wife and a gentle: 'Now, Bertie!'

Marina put her son's temper tantrums down to a lack of male
control and engaged Giles St Aubyn, son of Lord St Levan, as a

tutor. It turned out to be an inspired choice and Eddie greatly benefited by the companionship and enjoyed the walking tours in the holidays, organized by St Levan to give him some incognito freedom.

Young Edward not only had the turbulent Euro-Russian characteristics of his mother's family but flowing strongly in his veins was the blood of his Hanoverian ancestors, the much-maligned dynasty whose political, artistic and cultural achievements far outweighed their defects. From them the Duke of Kent not only inherited his love of music and the arts but he also greatly resembled the Hanoverian kings. As a baby, Chips Channon noted, he was 'curly haired and very red ... like all four Georges rolled into one'.

As both he and his mother had wished, Edward became a soldier and it was because of his military training that his life became entwined with Katharine Worsley's more standardized world. The Duke was posted to Catterick in 1956, just before his twenty-first birthday, and in the routine way in which the Worsleys' always entertained new officers at the camp, Prince Eddie was invited to Hovingham for lunch.

Kate had given up her job in London to help her mother who had been unwell and, in addition, suffered from severe arthritis. So she was one of the party of about a dozen people – four of them officers from Catterick – who sat down to lunch in the dining room of the Hall. It had originally been the State Bedroom, always included among the principal rooms in a country house until the end of the eighteenth century, and the two pillars at the far end once framed the great four-poster bed in which visiting dignitaries and royalty slept. When Thomas the Builder died in 1778 he was succeeded by his grandson Sir William Worsley, the first baronet, who dispensed with a State Bedroom and made it the family dining room. Now portraits of earlier Worsleys and some of the present generation hang on the walls and the room is furnished with fine Chippendale and Hepplewhite furniture.

As the daughter of the house, Kate sat next to the royal guest and it soon became evident that the two were extremely compatible. The Prince amused her by telling how a reporter and photographer had invaded his recent birthday party at Coppins attended by the Queen, the Duke of Edinburgh and most of the Royal Family, causing an unprecedented furore amongst security men.

Amongst the greetings he had on his birthday was one from Louis Armstrong whose music the Duke admired: 'To Black Jack – the sharpest little cat I know – Satch', went his message. After lunch Katharine showed their royal guest some of the treasures of Hovingham Hall including the craftsmanship of the London men – who normally worked on the royal palaces – who had travelled to Yorkshire to fashion the finest work in the house that Thomas Worsley built. Their names appear in the accounts, still preserved at Hovingham: Jonathan Rose, the plasterer; Moss, Kelsey and West, joiners who made eight mahogany windows and Corinthian caps to columns and pilasters; Jelfe the mason; Abbott the painter; Cobbett the glazier; Lawrence the wood-carver.

She showed him paintings of the Worsley family including one of herself by Sir Timothy Eden. Eddie stopped to admire it saying: 'But it doesn't do you justice, Miss Worsley.'

Hovingham Hall, in the comfortable, easy way of English country houses, seemed very much like Coppins – only grander – to the young Duke who was immensely bored by life at Catterick. A spark ignited that day which eventually developed into a loving and passionate relationship. 'I have never seen a couple so enchanted with one another,' said a friend soon after the initial attraction had flared into something more significant. Eddie was immediately captivated. He liked blue-eyed, effervescent blondes who were fun to be with yet remained kind and gentle. But royal romances need a helping hand and he asked his aunt, the late Princess Royal, to invite Kate to Harewood House for another luncheon party.

He discovered she was highly intelligent with an eloquent, expressive way of talking and a natural elegance, even in simple cotton dresses, of which his mother – always so exquisitely turned out – would be bound to approve. Kate noticed that her poodle, Charles, often snappish and possessive with his mistress's friends, liked Eddie and followed him around. It was surely a propitious sign in a relationship.

Yorkshire society hummed for the two years the regiment was at Catterick. The names of several daughters of stately homes were linked with Prince Eddie from time to time. But at the Bedale Hunt Ball he had eyes for no one but Kate Worsley and they danced nearly every dance together. Dressed in a pink and white Dresden shepherdess outfit, she made a delicate contrast to Eddie in flamboyant crimson Tudor costume and the press could not fail to pick up the story. The Duchess, surveying the papers next day, must have wondered how serious the friendship with Katharine Worsley was becoming.

At Sandhurst his lifestyle had worried Marina who could foresee some of her husband's early traits reappearing. His passion for fast cars was so like George and he had already crashed two of them. The friendship with Katharine, known to be a balanced, happy girl from an excellent background, might steady Eddie who was still inclined to be rash and headstrong.

He demonstrated this, in his mother's view, the Christmas after he had fallen in love with Kate when the Kents, along with the rest of the Royal Family, were the Queen's guests at Sandringham. Eddie had explained to Kate that he was expected to be there but would join her as soon as possible after Christmas Day. But when he mentioned to his mother that he was planning to ask the Queen's permission to leave Sandringham on Boxing Day, she was horrified and expressly forbade it. He usually listened dutifully but, this time, he defied her and spoke to the Queen. In her understanding way, she wished him 'God-speed' to Yorkshire.

Marina was both startled and worried by his rebellion and it may have influenced her later attitude to the couple's plans. Friends felt that her original feelings about the romance fluctuated. Marina, herself, was truly royal both by disposition and breeding. Through her Prince Edward was descended from Tsar Nicholas I of Russia and Charlemagne. On his father's side his ancestry goes back as far as King Harold and William the Conqueror, protagonists at the Battle of Hastings in 1066. Like Queen Mary, the Duchess believed in 'arranged marriages' but had

herself been fortunate that her own alliance with George, of
which everyone had so approved, had been a love match. But,
quoting her 'breeding will out' maxim, she always wanted her
children to marry royally. A crown – Scandinavian, perhaps? –
for Alexandra and, for Eddie, a princess. There were several who
would have been welcomed into the British Royal Family, forging
yet another dynastic alliance: Margrethe and Benedikte of
Denmark, Beatrix and Irene of the Netherlands and others of
lesser European royal families.

The Duchess invited Kate to Coppins for the weekend, giving
her a warm welcome but remaining somewhat distant from the
couple's obvious fondness for one another. They drove from
Yorkshire to Buckinghamshire in his Sunbeam Rapier 'K7' – he
was, at the time, seventh in line to the throne. On their way he
briefed Kate on the people she would be bound to meet. These
were, principally, 'Min' (the Duchess), and 'Maow' (his younger
brother). Princess Alexandra ('Pud' to the family because she had
been a podgy schoolgirl) was away in Germany with Prince Philip
at a family wedding.

The time had not yet come for Kate to call them by these
names. She was still very formal, curtseying to the Duchess as
she still did to Eddie in public.

Unexpectedly – because her son was so British – Kate found
Marina had a husky, foreign accent and was still amazingly attractive, as she remained all her life. She had invited some of her old
friends for tea that day who talked and talked, often breaking
into several languages until, with a word of apology, they recalled
the newcomer in their midst. It was a sophisticated, elegant
foreign atmosphere, set in the typically English surroundings of
Coppins. Only the exquisite silver and crystal and the incomparable Fabergé treasures set it apart from any other country
drawing-room.

All the Kents loved music and Kate saw there was an Ibeck
baby grand and a large Steinway, both of which she was destined
to play in the years ahead when she became chatelaine of Coppins.

Edward, that weekend, seems to have planned to introduce
Katharine to the most important members of his family. 'Aunt

Elizabeth', the Queen Mother, entertained them to tea at Royal
Lodge with Princess Margaret. They all chatted about Yorkshire
and the Queen Mother showed Kate round her magnificent
gardens which she had created with the late King.

Although there was no talk of marriage, it was certainly in the
air and obvious to all who met them that Eddie and Kate were
very much in love. The Queen Mother, always a sympathetic
ally in affairs of the heart for the royal or Bowes Lyon family,
had married a royal Duke herself but had certainly not rushed
into it. She had waited, as Kate was to do, until she was certain
she could accept all the changes life in the Royal Family would
mean.

The next day Princess Alexandra returned, bringing with her
the Duchess's sister, Princess Olga and her daughter Princess
Elizabeth. Eddie's sister and his girlfriend struck up an immediate
rapport which has since matured into an affectionate relationship
between sisters-in-law.

Throughout 1957, 'the two Ks' as friends called them were as
inseparable as his army duties allowed. Then, in the New Year,
came an occasion when the affair began to look really serious to
those outside the family. A dinner party was held at Coppins
before Princess Alexandra's twenty-first birthday party with the
Queen, Prince Philip, the Queen Mother – and Katharine
Worsley – present.

She was the only non-family guest invited to the dinner and
friends who arrived later for the dance, including a group of
officers from Catterick, were not slow to grasp the implication.
It was consolidated as Kate danced first with the Duke of Edinburgh, then talked to the Queen, and danced with the Duke of
Kent as often as his duties as host allowed.

Earlier Eddie had supervised doors being taken off their hinges
so that Alex could have the uninhibited conga line she wanted –
all over the ground floor of Coppins, to the music of Sid Phillip's
band, who had been asked to strike up with 'Downtown Strutter's
Ball'.

Later that year Eddie told his mother he wanted to marry
Kate – if possible before his regiment moved to Germany in the

early winter. Marina played for time, counselling patience to her son who was not inclined towards it.

Kate, herself, knew that she loved Eddie but was still uncertain that she could cope with the responsibilities her position as a royal Duchess would bring. It was an inner turmoil that Marina shrewdly sensed for she had grave doubts herself about Kate's ability to live behind the 'glass curtain' of royalty. Additionally Eddie's personality was such that he occasionally needed a really strong hand to curb his impetuosity and Marina felt that Kate's might be too gentle. But Marina did not then appreciate the strength of Katharine's character which her brother Marcus has mentioned. She can be both resolute and tenacious when necessary.

Marina talked with her niece, the Queen, and her sister-in-law, the Queen Mother. They both liked Katharine immensely but were concerned that Eddie, at only twenty-two, might not know his own mind. Marina remembered her own upbringing which had allowed her to blend easily with her royal in-laws. She had been reared by her mother, Princess Nicholas of Greece, to a life which, however informal in exile, was still, as Cecil Beaton put it: 'based on a deep regard for tradition and steeped in ritual'.

Knowing her mother's views, Alexandra, whilst hating to spoil their happiness, nevertheless warned Eddie and Kate: 'They'll argue delay – they always do.' Matters came to a head with the news that a date had been fixed for the transfer of the Duke's regiment to Germany for a two-year tour of duty.

Despite his sister's warning, Eddie had no doubt he could talk his family round, marry Kate and whisk her off to honeymoon in Germany. At a family conference at the Italian summer home of Prince and Princess Paul of Yugoslavia – the Duchess's sister Olga and her husband – the opposition proved formidable. Eddie was advised not to marry immediately and reminded that, like all those in line to the throne, he required the Queen's permission to wed under the Royal Marriages Act. She would, he knew, hesitate about giving her consent in view of his family's feelings. He had been the youngest royal Duke for generations when he succeeded his father at the age of seven; at nearly twenty-three he was still too young in experience, his elders stressed.

Katharine, who had been invited to cruise in the Mediterranean aboard Lord Astor's yacht, joined the Kents in Tuscany for a few days expecting that plans would have been made for their engagement. Instead she found a subdued and disappointed Eddie who told her: 'I'm afraid we shall have to wait.'

'Of course we could always elope,' he added hopefully, not really believing Katharine would agree to such precipitative action. She was too devoted to her own parents and becoming increasingly fond of Eddie's family to defy them to such an extent. In her own mind, also, there was still the niggling doubt about becoming a royal with all the strain of public engagements and other duties.

Reluctantly they both agreed to the postponement and total separation for a year so that they could be certain they wished to marry. They spent the last few weeks of their time together in Yorkshire, where Eddie celebrated his twenty-third birthday at Hovingham before the regiment left for Germany.

Kate flew off in another direction – across the Atlantic to stay with her brother John and his family in Toronto, Canada. There she planned to have a complete break and 'think things out'.

5

Between Two Worlds

Number 306 Vesta Drive, Forest Hill, in one of Toronto's pleasant suburbs, not far from the lakeside, was as different to ancient Hovingham Hall as could be. But Kate's brother John, his wife Carolyn and children Willa, then three, and the baby, Harry, provided a marvellous antidote to the uncertainties of the past year.

Kate found there was nothing so revitalizing as change when marking time and unsure of the future. The many new Canadian friends and the snow-covered countryside around Lake Ontario where, in summer, vines thrive along 25,000 acres of its banks, gave her a whole new perspective on life. It was just what her parents had hoped when they encouraged the visit.

She missed Eddie painfully but they had promised not to see each other or communicate before the year was up – a wretched arrangement which they did not – or could not – inflict on their own son when he fell in love. But Princess Alexandra wrote long letters to Kate, keeping her in touch with all the news and passed hers on to Edward who was spending most of his free time visiting motor racing tracks in Europe.

Katharine explored Toronto, gazing like all the other tourists at impressive CN, the Canadian National Tower which is slim and elegant, twice as tall as the Eiffel Tower. Beneath it modern buildings edge into the lakeside, the playground of the city where everyone skates in winter and sails, swims and picnics in summer.

In 1958 there was still a £50 travel allowance limit for Britons abroad and Kate could not do much more than window-shop in the old rival stores of Eaton's and Simpson's and the countless boutiques. But she bought small presents for her nephew and niece and the rest of the family as she planned to be home for Christmas.

An idea which would help fill up the long year that lay ahead was forming in her mind. Back at Hovingham over the holiday, she contacted a close friend Fiona Myddleton – now a lady-in-waiting to Princess Margaret and the wife of the Queen Mother's Comptroller, Sir Alistair Aird.

Kate's suggestion was that she and Fiona travel from her brother's in Canada, southwards to Mexico by greyhound bus. The idea was triggered off by Princess Alexandra's enthusiastic account of an official visit to Mexico with her mother. She had written a long, glowing letter to Kate about the trip which fuelled her urge to see something of the world whilst she was still free and unfettered by the protocol which dominates royal lives.

Again John and Carolyn asked her to stay and extended the invitation to Fiona also. Neither girl had enough money so, to finance the expedition, they both got jobs. Kate was employed by Henry Burks and Sons, the jewellers who are to Toronto what Asprey's or Garrard's are to London. Working as a shop girl in their gift department meant joining the commuting crowds making their way into the city and she really began to feel part of the busy working community. Selling high quality leather, English porcelain and other attractive goods was entertaining because she met so many people and she often looks back on the experience now as she buys gifts for family or friends in London.

When they had saved enough money – seventy dollars, they estimated – Kate and Fiona set off, waved goodbye on their sleek Greyhound bus by John, Carolyn and the children. They had picked the early autumn for the journey and found themselves travelling through a veritable wonderland of glowing colour in the tree-clad mountains and through the great canyons of the Rockies. They passed through places that had been visited only recently by the Queen and the Duke of Edinburgh when, locals joked, 'even the grizzly bears had been shampooed'.

In Vancouver, on Canada's West Coast, there were letters from England waiting – one from Alexandra telling Kate about a motor racing expedition with Eddie when he was on leave from Germany.

From Vancouver they bus-hopped to San Francisco, thence on via the fantastic Grand Canyon in Arizona, through the deserts of New Mexico and on to Mexico City. They had completed a journey of more than 10,000 miles by Greyhound bus.

Most visitors to Mexico City feel exhilarated by the combination of clear, brilliant light and the altitude. As she explored the city with its glass skyscrapers, exquisite churches, plazas, fountains and the sight and smell of masses of flowers everywhere, Kate knew that however vitalizing was the effect of 'the city in the sky', it was only a transitory euphoriant. For her, Mexico City was not a place to linger but only to halt for a while; to finally 'think things out', as she had promised herself when she began the journey.

Not everyone reaches a crossroads in their lives over 7,000 feet above sea level. But, before she turned for home along the Greyhound bus route to North America, Kate knew that it was decision time. Did she want to continue enjoying such freedom? Or should she marry the Duke of Kent and become a member of the Royal Family with all that entailed?

She would not have been human if she had not also wondered how Edward himself was reacting and whether he had survived the lonely test of separation. Royal Dukes are rare enough to be highly sought after and it would be easy to find a substitute for herself.

The answer came just before they climbed aboard the first of the succession of buses that would take them homewards via Texas, New Orleans and Washington. On that bright morning a huge bouquet of flowers was delivered to Kate. With it was a card bearing the one letter 'E'. He had not risked a message but the flowers told her all she wanted to know.

The reunion of Kate and Eddie came in November, soon

after his twenty-fourth birthday. He came home on leave from Germany and the Duchess invited Kate to dinner at Kensington Palace. Eddie was so excited at the prospect of seeing her again that he fell down a flight of steps and broke a bone in his foot.

But even the pain did not dull his eagerness to see her and in the face of their glowing looks and unquenchable happiness, Marina could no longer put up objections to the match. She still hesitated about setting a date for the formal engagement. One reason they must wait still longer, advised Marina, was that Princess Margaret had become secretly engaged to Antony Armstrong-Jones and that announcement would be made in the New Year. There could not be two royal weddings in the same year, decreed Marina. This prevarication was well-intentioned but for two young people in love it must have seemed an endless wait. Justification came, indirectly, some years later when the failure of Princess Margaret's marriage was blamed, by some, not only on incompatibility but the inescapable fact that both the Queen and Queen Mother had wanted to make up for their opposition that had resulted in her decision not to marry Group Captain Peter Townsend.

They agreed to the proposed marriage which the couple themselves had possibly not thought out carefully enough. 'It sounds hard-hearted but in a royal marriage it is best to be absolutely certain, especially if one partner is a commoner and does not understand the future commitments,' observed one of the Queen's family circle.

This was exactly Marina's view. With the worldly experience of an older generation she was only too aware that, at that time, divorce within the Royal Family was unthinkable. The Duchess wanted them to be very sure that the marriage would survive the undoubted strain of appearing on a public stage for much of their lives. Since then Princess Margaret's marriage has ended in divorce and Princess Anne has had to suffer the anguish and failure of a broken marriage also.

There are those within the Royal Family and the court who feel, even as the twenty-first century with all its changes approaches, that the old ways might still be best. An alliance with another royal means that both partners know exactly what they are letting themselves in for in today's media-dominated world. 'You think you know,' commented Princess Michael of Kent, 'but there is no way you could know what you are getting into.'

Princess Marina knew only too well and in her initial doubts about Kate's ability to readjust her life to fit in with the royal discipline, she must also have considered how she would stand up to the strain such a life imposes.

Stress takes its toll of royals and commoners alike and each member of the most publicized family in the world has evolved, for their own self-protection, ways of dealing with it. The Prince of Wales seeks solitude, believing that only a peaceful environment can produce the serenity he so desperately needs. He disappears into the Kalahari desert for a few days with his mentor, Sir Laurens van der Post; goes salmon fishing, standing in icy waters in his waders for hours on end; spent three days living with a crofter's family in the Hebrides or works as a farmhand on his own Duchy of Cornwall property. These breaks from his own everyday life of speech-making and endless public appearances give him tranquillity and contentment and as he said after one such retreat from palace discipline: 'Being here has restored my sanity.'

Of all the rest of the family, perhaps only the Duchess of Kent, with her sensitive awareness developed through stress and personal affliction, might understand his profound conviction unleashed upon an unreceptive audience in Canada that 'as modern man we have lost that sense of meaning within nature's scheme of things which helps to preserve that delicate balance between the world of the instinctive unconscious and that of the conscious'. The Princess of Wales restores her equilibrium by getting up to the elbows in Fairy Liquid, washing up the dishes at a private dinner party – 'The beautiful Princess wants to become Cinderella again for the evening,' quipped a fellow guest who had wandered into the kitchen … A fellow shopper in a West Country branch of The Body Shop found Diana standing in the queue beside her, with Princes William and Harry, buying shampoo for her husband and oatmeal and honey face cream for herself. It is her way of unwinding; doing the things that were normal before she exchanged a number nine bus for her bridal glass coach and working girl anonymity for the glare of the world stage as a future Queen.

Her mother-in-law, the Queen, has never apparently been over sensitive about her God-given task and the lack of privacy it entails that so bothers Diana. But she has, over the years, worked out her own ways of relaxing when she and the Duke of Edinburgh behave much like their mutual great-great-grandparents, Victoria and Albert. Only they have modern log cabins to replace the small stone bothies where Queen Victoria and her Consort played at being ordinary. Ex-Prime Minister Harold Wilson's story of his wife Mary helping the Queen with the washing-up, after tea in her small 'picnic' cottage on the Balmoral estate, illustrates her propensity to play ordinary woman. 'The Queen is a "manqué" housewife' as her cousin Lady Elizabeth Anson put it.

But it has the same unreal quality about it as the two small princesses – Elizabeth and Margaret Rose – playing in the Welsh cottage of their childhood with a future ahead of them that did not include keeping house.

Prince Philip finds painting and wildlife photography helps to dispel his frustrations with a prince's life. He spends hours on the Scottish moors with the Queen, sitting on a rug beside him, reading whilst her husband pursues his hobbies. The results are displayed in the royal homes beside the Old Masters. Only in Craigowan House, on the Balmoral estate, do they get unceremoniously moved when Prince Charles stays there. He dislikes his father's modern efforts and replaces them with Queen Victoria's gloomy paintings of antlered stags and heavy mountain landscapes. When Prince Philip, in his turn, stays at Craigowan for the shooting, his own pictures go back on the wall.

For the Duke and Duchess of Kent, it is music that relaxes them most. They are passionately fond of opera and are regular visitors to the Royal Box at Covent Garden whenever it is available. They spend the evening totally absorbed in the performance and there are few pleasures they enjoy more. Music has been an integral part of their life together; their mutual love of it was one of the factors that initially drew them together and it has nourished their relationship through the years, particularly in the dark time of Kate's illness when the test of having to wait before they married must have seemed infinitesimal by comparison with the hurdle they encountered after sixteen years of marriage.

But, back in 1960, it was patience that was needed most. It turned out that the announcement of Princess Margaret's engagement had to wait also, but only for a few weeks until after the birth of Prince Andrew, the Queen's third child. The royals, Katharine learnt, have to queue up on these occasions so that announcements do not run into and detract from each other.

The months dragged on and still they had to wait for one reason or another. It was eighteen months later that their own engagement was announced on 8 March 1961. During that time Marina coached her future daughter-in-law in royal ways until she began to feel more confident of her position in the new world she would be entering when she married the Duke of Kent. The Duchess was as much a stickler for protocol as her mentor Queen Mary, and insisted on nothing less than perfection. Lady Elizabeth Anson, the Queen Mother's great-niece, told me once how she had come up against Marina's inflexible determination to observe protocol, however informal the situation. They were on their way to Amsterdam for the wedding of Princess Beatrix at which Lady Elizabeth was a bridesmaid. She mentioned to Marina that curtsies were not acceptable to the Dutch Queen who was very informal. Marina replied stiffly that she and her party represented Britain and curtsies would be *de rigueur*. On another occasion, soon after Princess Alexandra's wedding to the Hon (now Sir) Angus Ogilvy, it came to her mother's ears that he was introducing his wife as 'Alexandra' at their dinner parties. This was altogether too casual for Marina and she insisted he always said: 'Her Royal Highness Princess Alexandra.'

The Queen Mother, always so understanding, was particularly kind saying to the rest of the family: 'We must do everything to help Katharine get to know us.' She invited them to a dance at Clarence House soon after their reunion, given as a private celebration for Margaret and Tony. It was also an even more private one for Kate and Eddie who would have to keep their love a secret much longer. But few people were fooled that night as Kate, in an exquisite ball gown, danced with the Duke beneath the Waterford crystal chandeliers in the Queen Mother's drawing room at Clarence House to the hit tune of the moment: 'What do you want to make those eyes at me for?'

Then, just a couple of days before Eddie returned to Germany, the Queen threw a party at Buckingham Palace to welcome Princess Alexandra home from her first big overseas tour. Again Kate was invited, along with several friends of the young Kents, among them Angus Ogilvy who two years later became engaged to Alexandra.

The Duke's return to Germany was brief for on 9 December he returned again on special leave so that he could be introduced as a peer to the House of Lords. Above in a gallery, the Duchess of Kent, Princess Alexandra, Prince Michael and Katharine Worsley watched the ceremony.

Five months later she was a guest at the wedding of Princess Margaret to Antony Armstrong-Jones, later Lord Snowdon, in Westminster Abbey.

As the time drew nearer to her own wedding her future mother-in-law continued to instruct the soon to be Duchess in all the unseen pitfalls a born-royal becomes accustomed to from childhood but which can be daunting to a beginner. Handshaking is an art, she learnt. People tend to give the royal hand a hearty shake which can become intensely painful after the first few dozen. The Duchess of York always has to wear gloves because she has sensitive hands but the Princess of Wales – who hates them – usually manages without. In Kate's early days as a royal, three decades ago, gloves were still obligatory. It was just one of the lessons to be learnt because, as she was beginning to discover, she was not only marrying a man but a family and a way of life.

Queen Mary always used to advise a new princess to read approved royal biographies, so that she could have an instant lesson in royal history and this the Duchess suggested Kate should do, just as she herself had done.

Above all the kind, caring, friendly girl who loved chatting to people had to learn not to be too familiar with those she met. Nowadays she has achieved a warm, approachable compromise which blends smoothly with her own inherent dignity.

But behind it all there is an aloofness, barely discernible but nevertheless there; the armour her mother-in-law taught her to wear as protection against presumption and which, she has since learnt, can sometimes be all too necessary.

Kate and Eddie would like to have been married in the small All Saints church at Hovingham like all the Worsley brides; Marina wanted the wedding in Westminster Abbey where she and George had been married. But, if she could not be wed in Hovingham, Kate asked that their marriage be solemnized in York Minster because it was the heart of Yorkshire and meant so much to the Worsleys.

The Queen approved this plan and, certainly, it suited her very well, giving the North of her Kingdom a royal wedding for the first time since Edward III was married to Philippa of Hainault in York Minster in 1328.

Edward, twenty-five in October 1960, was nearing the end of his stint in Germany and began to take on royal duties. He was appointed an aide to the Queen for the State Visit of the King and Queen of Nepal and, the following year, represented the Queen at the Independence ceremonies in Sierra Leone. At a royal house-party over Christmas, 1960, the Queen conferred upon him the dignity of a Knight Grand Cross of the Royal Victorian Order and invested him with the insignia of that order. Soon afterwards the Duke asked the Queen's formal permission to marry Katharine Worsley which she granted 'with great pleasure'. The long wait was almost over.

He also obtained the Queen's permission to leave Sandringham early so that he could join Kate in Yorkshire as soon as possible. But, having waited so long, Edward now showed a romantic, ritualistic streak worthy of his Romanov ancestors. He waited until New Year's Day, an important event in the Russian calendar, with 'the ring burning a hole in my pocket', before he formally proposed. He chose the background of the impressive library at Hovingham with its collection of fine books lining the walls, the warm colours of their bindings mellowed with age and use through the centuries by generations of Worsleys.

Then he produced the ring – a magnificent sapphire flanked by diamonds – family stones of sentimental value which followed the royal fashion of choosing sapphires, said to be a symbol of love and purity, for their engagement rings. In 1934 Marina of Greece was given a square Kashmir sapphire with a diamond on each side by Prince George, Duke of Kent. The Queen's ring is also a sapphire surrounded by diamonds which had belonged to her mother-in-law Princess Andrew of Greece. The Queen Mother received a Kashmir sapphire surrounded by diamonds on her engagement to the then Duke of York, later King George VI, as did Princess Alice when she accepted Henry, Duke of Gloucester. In the younger generation Princess Alexandra also has a sapphire and diamond engagement ring and her younger brother Prince Michael followed family tradition by giving Marie-Christine a sapphire and diamond ring inherited from his mother. In the still younger generation Princess Anne and the Princess of Wales both have sapphire and diamond engagement rings. But the present Duke of York gave his Sarah something different – a magnificent ruby 'to go with her hair'.

On New Year's Day, 1961, Kate was proudly wearing her ring when her parents entered the room just before lunch. Sir William took one look at their faces and produced the champagne he had prudently chilled for the pre-lunch drinks. Just as the family had toasted Kate's birth almost twenty-eight years before, they celebrated her engagement to the Duke of Kent as the pictures of Worsley ancestors looked down.

Early in February the Duke took up his new staff job at the War Office, as it was then known, the first member of his family to work there this century. He set off for Whitehall each day in sober suit and bowler hat, leaving his mother's apartments at Kensington Palace in a small Austin Seven, less conspicuous than his fast Jaguar.

For the Duchess, soon to be Princess Marina of Kent – a title she preferred to 'Dowager' – it was a bitter-sweet period of adjustment. When Eddie married she ceased to be *the* Duchess of Kent and chatelaine of Coppins, the much loved home that had been left to the eldest son under the terms of his father's will.

Since his death the four Kents – Min, Eddie, Pud and Maow – had become extremely close, the mother ultra-protective of her children and they more warmly vigilant of her well-being than is customary in a two-parent family.

Deeply aware that her life would never be quite the same again, Marina plunged into preparations for the wedding, asking her own principal designer John Cavanagh to design Kate's wedding dress. Retired now, and living in Wandsworth, he remembers being summoned by the Duchess to Kensington Palace for the initial discussions. Greatly admiring his royal client he was thrilled to be asked to make the bridal gown of the future Duchess. Marina was, according to Cavanagh, 'sheer magic and always remained my dream woman, personifying superb elegance. Later on she was often my inspiration.' On this occasion the dress he created, based on the ideas of both Katharine and the Duchess, was certainly inspired and is still memorable to those who saw it.

Like all royal weddings, so magnificent on the day in the solemn, awe-inspiring setting of Minster, Abbey or cathedral, the behind-the-scenes details caused some amusement and not a little apprehension to the participants. For such impressive settings a longer than usual train is necessary if the effect is not to be dwarfed by the proportions of the building.

In a small fitting-room the fifteen-foot-long train looked immense and how, queried Marina, would it react when Kate knelt during the ceremony? Unruffled, Cavanagh produced some telephone directories so that she could practise there and then. They also rehearsed how the bride would manage the train when the moment came to curtsey to the Queen at the beginning of her walk back down the aisle. Again the designer had the answer, suggesting Katharine should half-turn towards the Queen, then step back to release the tautness of the shimmering material in the train. They tried it out with Cavanagh taking her arm and playing the part of bridegroom. Kate was relieved to see that it worked – if only she could remember it on the day.

The formal engagement was announced on 8 March 1961: 'It is with the greatest pleasure that the Duchess of Kent announces the betrothal of her elder son, Prince Edward, Duke of Kent, to Katharine, only daughter of Sir William and Lady Worsley, to which union the Queen has gladly given her consent.'

Three weeks before the wedding Marina and her two eldest children made a pilgrimage to the late Duke's memorial on the Hill of Morven near Wick. They went on foot to the spot near the Eagle's Rock where the plane had crashed. There a five-foot Celtic Cross commemorated all those who had died on 25 August 1942. At such an important moment in their son's life, Marina felt the need to share it with his father in the only way possible.

6

The White Rose

Thousands of the traditional white roses of York – para-doxically grown in Leicestershire because Yorkshire could not supply enough of them – decorated the vast Minster. Their fragrance wafting the scent of an English summer garden through the congregation which included three Queens and the heirs to six European royal houses among the other royals and notabilities present.

As Walter Bagehot, the Victorian writer and authority on constitutional monarchy, once observed, a royal wedding 'rivets mankind'. It was only the wedding of the Queen's cousin on that June day in 1961 but he was a royal prince, grandson of a King and the ceremony was headline news. Or as Bagehot put it: 'a princely marriage is the brilliant edition of a universal fact – brilliant, because a princely marriage is compact of pageantry; universal, because marriage is a common human experience ...'

Journalists from all over the world, including forty-six television crews, converged on York and Hovingham, dubbing the occasion 'The Wedding of the White Rose'. It was only one of several irresistible angles to this royal wedding. The entire city of York was *en fête* for the marriage of Lord Protector Oliver Cromwell's descendant to a scion of the executed King Charles I.

The Queen and other members of the Family had slept in the royal train overnight on the outskirts of the city of which King George VI once said: 'The history of York is the history of

England.' Much of that long and living chronicle lies buried within the venerable stones of the medieval masterpiece that rose on the site of the wooden church built for the baptism of Edwin, King of Northumbria, in 627.

The present cathedral Church of St Peter was conceived by Archbishop Walter de Gray in 1216 and its royal associations began when King Edward III was married there in 1328, at the age of fifteen, in a dynastic alliance with Philippa of Hainault. His younger son, Prince William of Hatfield, is entombed in the Minster; his effigy showing a young man resting against a crouched lion is in the north aisle of the choir. Later in his reign when York became the capital of England in the war against the Scots, Edward governed the country from within its walls and the Minster became, virtually, his parish church.

In choosing it for her wedding Kate undoubtedly did so for personal reasons but she also saved the Crown a considerable amount of money. The Queen inevitably picks up the bill for the weddings of close relatives because of the immense expense involved.

In York there was none of the costly pageantry involved in processions of royal carriages from palace to church with their glittering escort of outriders. A London wedding would have involved more police manpower, troops on ceremonial duty and much else besides. In a big Westminster Abbey wedding the Lord Chamberlain and the Palace press office is normally totally involved because it is so essential that everything runs smoothly. For Kate's wedding, Princess Marina's office coped magnificently with the major arrangements with only occasional reference to the Lord Chamberlain's office. Oliver Worsley, Kate's bachelor brother, arranged most efficiently the reception at Hovingham Hall. But when it came to Princess Alexandra's turn in April 1963, Princess Marina had her way and the wedding had all the hallmarks of a traditional royal ceremony with the Queen sparing no expense to make it so.

But Kate and her family wanted her wedding to reflect their background in Yorkshire and the places she loved best. So the atmosphere, although ritualistic and formal, was also that of a country wedding with villagers from Hovingham sitting opposite the grandest names in Europe. Despite the distinguished guest list it was, nevertheless, a get-together of parents, friends and relatives – more like the royal weddings of old which were quieter and more private than today.

Westminster Abbey, in fact, has only become fashionable in this century as the venue for most royal weddings. The future King George VI and Queen Elizabeth were married there as were Prince George and Princess Marina, the Queen (then Princess Elizabeth), Princess Margaret, Princess Anne, Princess Alexandra and Prince Andrew. Only the Prince of Wales broke the mould – choosing St Paul's Cathedral, possibly because his bride's divorced parents had been married in the Abbey and he considered it inappropriate.

Queen Victoria, daughter of the first Duke of Kent (of the new creation) was married, wearing white satin and Honiton lace, in the Chapel Royal, St James's Palace where, one hundred and forty nine years later, her commoner great-great-great-great-grand-son – the son of Kate and Eddie's eldest son, George – was christened. The shy Queen would have much preferred her wedding to be completely private in a room at Buckingham Palace. But her Prime Minister, Lord Melbourne, overruled her and insisted the wedding was more public. However, when her son, the future Edward VII, was married in St George's Chapel, Windsor, the widowed Queen, in perpetual mourning for Prince Albert, was as reclusive as she wished. She watched the ceremony from Queen Catherine of Aragon's closet where she was safe from observers. When the Queen approved Katharine's wish to be married in York Minster, she may well have remembered the many royal associations and the special place it occupied in the lives of past royals, particularly King Edward III, a great warrior whose rule established prosperity and stability in medieval England.

Now, just as sap rises in the ancient wood of a centuries-old tree, the Sovereign, surrounded by her family, sat once again in the Minster at the marriage of another royal Edward. They sat beneath a soaring fourteenth-century window of exquisite stained glass that would have likely graced the earlier royal wedding. It is one of the great treasures of the Minster which has incomparable stained glass including the oldest piece in the world – a twelfth-century panel in the north aisle of the nave.

The thirteen bells of the south-west tower began to peal an hour before the ceremony, as Katharine finished dressing in her bedroom at Hovingham Hall. Earlier all the small calamities that arise on such occasions duly appeared. Willa – John and Caroline's daughter who had come from Canada to be a bridesmaid – went to bed with a temperature the night before and alarmed everyone. In the morning, as Kate looked out of her window, the rain-filled clouds over the marquees that had flowered overnight on the lawns looked ominously persistent.

It was unpredictable weather, more like April than June. But, like all the best fairy stories, as she stepped into her shining silk gown, the skies cleared and the small bridesmaid was bright and chirpy again, ready to join the seven other bridesmaids, headed by eleven-year-old Princess Anne and three pages who attended the bride. Kate looked white and tremulous as she descended the wide staircase of the Hall as so many Worsley brides had done since Thomas the Builder designed it three centuries before.

But as she drove with her father in the glass-topped car lent by the Queen, through the familiar villages where well-wishers waited to greet her, a little colour crept back into her face. Occasionally she put a hand up towards the row of fine pearls her parents had given her as a wedding present and the diamond tiara, once Queen Mary's, that had been Princess Marina's gift.

Her bridegroom and his brother and best man, Prince Michael, had their share of good wishes when they drove into York earlier from Nawton Hall where they had been staying with Princess Marina's friends, the Earl and Countess of Feversham.

As Kate and her father approached the flag-decked city, excited crowds were in holiday mood. Many of them had waited all night and now they stretched back across the pavements and hung from windows. The clamour of the great bells, which could be heard all over York, was almost drowned by cheers as the bride and her father passed by; a sound that travelled before them and alerted those waiting in the Minster that the bride would soon be there.

The venerable pews bloomed with myriad colours as women guests displayed their finery. On the bride's side were the summery silks and linens of Yorkshire friends and relatives; their menfolk in morning dress and toppers on the floor by their feet. On the groom's side was the largest assembly of British and foreign royalty assembled since Elizabeth II's own wedding in 1947. Among them was Queen Victoria-Eugenie of Spain – 'cousin Ena' – granddaughter of Queen Victoria whose 1906 wedding to King Alfonso XIII in Madrid was marred by a bomb thrown at the bridal procession, resulting in the bride's white satin gown being spattered with blood. Her mind obviously far from the mischance at her own wedding, the Queen was happily nodding to friends and relatives around her and afterwards summed up everyone's feelings at the marriage of her Kent cousin to the daughter of a Yorkshire country squire: 'Young Katharine was simply adorable, glittering and very blonde.'

Among other foreign guests, all inter-related, were the Duke of Gerona, the Count of Barcelona and his son (now the King of Spain), Crown Prince (now ex-King) Constantine of Greece and his sister Princess Sophie (now Queen of Spain – she met her future husband at the wedding), Prince Harald of Norway, Princess Margrethe (now Queen) of Denmark, Prince Charles of Luxembourg, Princess Irene of the Netherlands, Prince and Princess George of Denmark, Prince Frederick of Prussia, Princess Ileana of Romania and several of the Yugoslav royal family.

The Queen, in pale lilac, headed the British royals with Prince Philip, the Prince of Wales, the Queen Mother, Princess Margaret (expecting her first baby) and Antony Armstrong-Jones (not yet created Lord Snowdon). Also present in the family party were the late Duke of Gloucester and his Duchess (now Princess Alice) and the late Princess Royal with her sons.

The bridegroom's mother, so soon to be Princess Marina again – as she was when she arrived in Britain to marry in 1934 – wore a breathtaking John Cavanagh creation of champagne silk organdy embroidered with diamanté gold and silver thread. A cartwheel halo of matching osprey feathers swathed her sleek dark hair and, as she always did, she stole the fashion honours completely. By her side sat Princess Alexandra, glowing in azalea pink organdy, also made by Cavanagh. Sitting alongside were Prince and Princess Paul of Yugoslavia, Marina's brother-in-law and sister.

Trumpeters of the Duke's regiment, the Royal Scots Greys, had sounded the first fanfare which heralded the arrival of the Queen, the Duke of Edinburgh in the uniform of a Field Marshal and their son Prince Charles. Their procession was led by the Gentlemen-at-Arms, the residentiary canons and the Dean and Archbishop of York. Outside the bridesmaids and pages waited, the girls in 'Kate Greenaway' dresses of white organza with posies of roses and tiny rosebuds in their hair.

As they waited for the bride a selection of music, carefully chosen by the two music-loving families, was played on the Minster's famous organ: Bach's Prelude and Fugue in G; Herbert Howell's Siciliano for a High Ceremony and the Prelude on 'Rhosymedre' by Ralph Vaughan Williams. Kate had wanted to include the forty-fifth psalm in the wedding ceremony because it was by a Yorkshire composer. Then she realized it contained the words 'Forget also thine own people and thine father's house' ... and decided she could not possibly have it.

Finally, just three minutes late, came a second fanfare as the bride, leaning on her father's arm, came through the great archway of the West Door. They stood there for a moment, framed within its shelter, as 630 years before another royal bride, Philippa of Hainault, paused briefly before she entered the Minster.

Somehow the timelessness of the largest gothic cathedral north of the Alps, in the centre of one of Britain's best preserved medieval cities, seemed to link those two weddings. For a brief moment, as the light filtered through the stained-glass windows and caught the diamonds on her narrow bandeau tiara, Kate could have been a bride of medieval times walking towards her destiny at the High Altar.

Her gown, made of 237 yards of shimmering white silk gauze, had a distinctly medieval look with its softly rounded neckline and narrow standaway collar. Woven into the material was iridescent thread that gleamed like tiny diamonds. Three wedding veils had been made – one for rehearsals, one for the ceremony and another for emergencies and the photographic session after the wedding. Unlike most royal brides, Kate's face was covered by an additional filmy panel of veiling, held in place by diamond pins, when she arrived for the wedding. The unusual and effectively simple bandeau of diamonds – which when it belonged to Queen Mary had been far more elaborate with oval cabochan emeralds along the top – completed the look of a bygone age.

At the foot of the altar steps stood the Duke of Kent in the ceremonial uniform of the Royal Scots Greys – scarlet jacket, tight blue trousers with yellow stripes – which he had obtained special permission to wear as it was forty years out of date. Across his chest he wore the dark blue sash of the Royal Victorian Order.

When Edward had taken his place, turning to smile at his relatives, it was not only his mother who caught her breath for a moment. His resemblance to his father was so striking and apparent to all of the generations who remembered him. 'It could have been George standing there,' said Lord Mountbatten afterwards. Beside Edward stood his younger brother Prince Michael, in the ceremonial uniform of an officer cadet at Sandhurst, who was his best man.

The Duke half turned at Katharine's entrance and, as a commentator put it, 'a friendly chuckle ran through the congregation at the bridegroom's expression of delight when she made her entry'.

The organ played 'O praise ye the Lord' as the bride's procession moved slowly down the aisle tailing off into some appealing disarray as the youngest of the eleven child attendants, bewildered by the impressive setting and the many staring faces, began to trail out of line. Tranquil and beautiful, Katharine inclined slightly towards her seventy-one-year-old father and both 'gave an impression of touching devotion' in the words of historian Roger Fulford.

The bride had asked that the 1928 service could incorporate the word 'obey' from the 1662 prayer book and, in the emotive moments as they exchanged their vows, tears glimmered in the eyes of both bride's and bridegroom's mothers – as inevitable a reaction in a royal wedding as in any other.

Marina's old friend, Noël Coward, also found himself stirred by the wedding. 'Everything about the ceremony was very moving,' he wrote in his diary. 'Prince Eddie looked so exactly like his father. The Duchess's looks, poise and glorious dignity were infinitely touching.'

Princess Marina appeared the more emotional of the two mothers as the ceremony proceeded, dabbing her eyes with a lace-edged handkerchief, and Alexandra occasionally turned to her with a gentle smile as if willing her to composure.

Bringing yet another personal touch to the wedding, the bride had requested one of her favourite prayers, ascribed to St Francis of Assisi, which Princess Marina liked so much she afterwards learnt it by heart:

> Lord make us the Instruments of thy will;
> where there is hate may we bring love;
> where there is offence may we bring pardon;
> where there is discord may we bring peace;
> where there is error may we bring truth;
> where there is doubt may we bring faith;
> where there is dismay may we bring joy;
> where there is darkness may we bring light.

After the marriage ceremony when the Duke placed a simple gold ring on Katharine's finger, and the signing of the register, a final fanfare from the trumpeters preceded the bride and bridegroom's procession down the aisle.

But just as she walked slowly past the altar, the long flowing train caught on the steps. Near disaster was averted by the quick wits of an usher who released it as Kate stood, very still, smiling at her husband. The music of Widor's Toccata in F resounded through the Minster as they passed the eight statues of the Duke's ancestors – from William the Conqueror to Henry VI – on the fifteenth-century organ screen. Then the new Duchess made her deep and graceful curtsey to the Queen, an obeisance accomplished without further problems with her train.

Outside the Minster, brother officers made a ceremonial arch of swords as the thirteen bells pealed forth to celebrate the wedding of a Yorkshire lass and a royal Duke, just as they had rung sixteen years before in May 1945, when Kate visited York on Victory-in-Europe Day.

The Hovingham lawns where most of the century's most eminent cricketers have played looked particularly festive later that afternoon as two thousand guests in wedding finery enjoyed a champagne and strawberries-and-cream reception. Large marquees and bright umbrellas above the many small tables decorated with posies of flowers contrasted with the beauty of the herbaceous borders not yet as brilliant with colour as they would be later in the year. But, as if to honour Hovingham's own 'White Rose', the roses were superb – bringing compliments from the Royal Family's most accomplished gardener, the Queen Mother, who has always considered the rose as her favourite flower.

There were all the small human cameos that weave a kaleidoscope of memories into wedding days. Cousin Ena, the exiled Queen of Spain, chatting to her grandson the Infante Juan Carlos, Prince of the Asturias and now King of Spain. With them a laughing, slender girl who was a princess in her own right – Sofia of Greece who became the bride of Juan Carlos and Queen of Spain, after meeting her husband at Hovingham. Prince Michael, more relaxed now his duties were over, was gallantly protective of his mother, constantly at her side and laughing as she and Eddie used, in Hugo Vickers's words, their secretary Sir Philip Hay as 'a mobile human ash-tray'.

Lady Worsley, mother of the bride, flushed and happy, thoroughly enjoying herself now the emotive part of the wedding was over, forgot to curtsey to her daughter who was now a royal Duchess and a Princess of the Realm; a fact that did not go unnoticed by the eagle-eyed 'old guard' of palace officials present, among them the Queen's press secretary Sir Richard Colville who was heard shouting orders at Princess Marina's friend Cecil Beaton who was taking the photographs.

The bridesmaids and pages, 'full to the gills' with the strawberry-and-cream tea Oliver had provided, grew more rumbustious and high-spirited as was inevitable until, at last, the Queen, who had been enjoying herself hugely meeting all the long-lost relatives, decided it was time to make tracks for the royal train, still waiting at York to take them home.

It was the happiest of parties with friendly Yorkshire neighbours and friends mixing easily with the many royals present. There were no speeches which may have disappointed Prince Philip who enjoys making his own witty contributions on family occasions but greatly relieved Prince Michael, the best man. Nevertheless he performed his duty of toasting the small, giggling – and by now thoroughly exuberant – bridesmaids with diffident charm.

The festivities continued well into the small hours, as all the many helpers stayed on to be entertained, in their turn, by the Worsley family with a traditional Boar's Head banquet and more champagne. The bride and groom were having a small party of their own as an aircraft of the Queen's Flight flew them to their honeymoon in the Queen Mother's Scottish home, Birkhall near Balmoral. The Queen had noticed that they had been so busy meeting guests, they had not eaten much at the reception and thoughtfully provided three bottles of vintage champagne and smoked salmon sandwiches which they shared with the crew.

Birkhall, named after the birch trees which surround it, is a favourite royal home and the perfect place for a honeymoon as the Queen and the Duke of Edinburgh had found in 1947. 'The nicest place in the world', the Queen had told Kate and she certainly found it so. The whitewashed Jacobite house still has the happiest of memories when they return to visit the Queen Mother during her Scottish holiday.

The Duke had known the house all his life and was longing to show his wife some of his favourite places in the beautiful, secluded surroundings through which the River Muick tumbles towards the Dee and where, the previous month, the Queen Mother had been fishing for salmon as she usually does in May. The Royal Family has always loved Birkhall. Eddie could remem-

ber staying in a caravan there before the Queen Mother added
another wing to accommodate more guests. Birkhall was part of
all their childhoods – Prince Charles learnt to cast a fly from his
grandmother's sloping lawns – and it has become a favourite
honeymoon spot.

Princess Alice of Athlone, granddaughter of Queen Victoria,
summed up everything the royals feel about Birkhall: 'Here we
spent some of the happiest days of our lives. It was a small place in
those days. We loved the sloping garden full of fruit and sweet-
peas and, at the bottom, a chain bridge, heavenly to jump upon,
which spanned the rushing little Muick where we loved to play.'

All around are woodlands and, beyond, the moors where
the Duke's great-great-grandparents, Queen Victoria and Prince
Albert, enjoyed walking in all weathers. Like them Kate and
Eddie walked their dogs – Charles and Columbus who had flown
to Scotland with them – through the woods, over the heather-
clad hills and on the shores of the loch where the Royal Family
picnic near Queen Victoria's cottage.

After a relaxing fortnight at Balmoral they flew south to
Majorca where in the north-east peninsula of Formentor the
beautiful Villa Quiros, lent by Sir Whitney Straight, awaited
the second stage of their honeymoon. There, surrounded by
mountains and forests, on the edge of a craggy bay, they spent
an idyllic three weeks: sunbathing, swimming, and water skiing.
Kate, her skin unused to so much sun, had a mild attack of
sunstroke and had to stay in the shade for a while.

As honeymooners do they rejoiced in the present; talked a
little of the past and looked forward to the future. Unlike most
newlyweds, their first home was not a problem of saving up and
furnishing gradually. Princess Marina had insisted that Coppins
was theirs alone and she left it exactly as it had always been when
she left to make her permanent home with Princess Alexandra
and Prince Michael – when he was on leave – at Kensington
Palace. Kate and Eddie had asked her to stay on in the home she
had known for so many years but she refused, saying: 'It is the
only sensible thing to do.'

7

First Home

Coppins, the home the Duke of Kent had known all his life and inherited on his twenty-first birthday, was waiting for them when they returned from honeymoon, its front door festooned with a banner which read: 'Welcome Home'. The house had become part of the family when it was left to the late Duke by his 'Aunt Toria', the outspoken Princess Victoria, daughter of King Edward VII and Queen Alexandra. She and her brother King George V were devoted to each other and it was their habit to talk on the telephone every day.

The Princess, whose vocabulary was peppered with oaths gleaned originally in the stables, usually began with: 'Hello is that you – you old bugger?' On one occasion she had not yet been connected to the King and when she produced the usual greeting, an embarrassed operator said: 'One moment, please. His Majesty is not yet on the line.'

Princess Victoria had always been fond of her nephew who amused her with his racy anecdotes and wicked stories about the rest of the family. He always sought out some rare gossip to regale her with when he visited Coppins and had made a point of driving Marina down to meet his aunt.

When she died the Princess left 'Georgie' her cream-washed Victorian villa in Buckinghamshire. Her bequest was more than welcome as the Duke and Duchess were looking for a country home now they had a baby son, Prince Edward.

George, who took after Queen Mary in his love of furniture and fine art, also had a talent for interior decorating and, from the first, Marina left everything to him. He transformed the Edwardian and Victorian gloom that had dominated Coppins, choosing new colour schemes and furnishings in the lightest pastels. 'I let him make all the decisions over furniture and decorations. He has a wonderful sense of colour and design', Marina told Lady Airlie, Queen Mary's lady-in-waiting.

'Chips' Channon praised the Duke's talent when he visited them, writing in his diary '... the rooms now glow with luxe and gaiety. It is entirely due to Prince George who has transformed it and now thinks of little else ....' It was not surprising that the old house took on a new life under his skilful hands and Marina gracefully relinquished other wifely duties such as choosing their menus and speaking to the chef. After one dinner party she admitted to Lady Airlie: 'I am really a very bad hostess. I must confess that I didn't know what we were going to eat tonight until the food appeared. George chose the dinner and the wine – and the flowers and everything else. He enjoys doing it, and so I always leave the household affairs to him.'

Coppins, therefore, still reflected Prince George's personality although he, himself, was long gone from it, and the house meant a great deal to the Kent family. Like all new wives taking over from a previous chatelaine, Kate moved cautiously and diplomatically when it came to changing anything in the house. Princess Marina had moved out, not without regret, to live permanently with Princess Alexandra – and Michael when he was home on leave – in the apartment in Kensington Palace. But she would be a frequent and welcome visitor when Eddie and Kate had settled in.

So, essentially, the house remained the same showing, like most royal homes, that beauty and shabbiness are compatible if blended with flair. Indeed, in their private rooms, the Royal Family find anything too perfect distinctly bourgeois. A touch of shabbiness spells homeliness, particularly if the object is part of a well-loved room. The Queen Mother was so reluctant to part with the time-worn covers of two easy chairs at Royal Lodge that, in the end, the Queen and Princess Margaret clubbed together to buy new ones. Then their mother was delighted, saying to guests: 'Don't you think they are charming?'

Kate loved the drawing room at Coppins where light streamed in from the gardens picking out the colours of the chintz which George had chosen so carefully. Antique chairs fashioned by craftsmen shone with years of careful polishing although the colours were fading on the upholstery.

When Katharine had first seen it, exquisite Fabergé ornaments highlighted the room along with George's collection of snuff boxes, Chinese jade, drawings, lithographs and paintings. But most of these were auctioned before her wedding to Eddie, to give Marina some much-needed liquidity.

In the dining room there was the gleam of shining Georgian silver and oil paintings of royal ancestors looked down from the walls. The table could seat fourteen and had seen some of the most sparkling, witty dinner parties of the pre-war era when George and Marina had entertained a select mish-mash of royal and show business personalities.

The dogs, Columbus – who already knew it well – and Charles, were well settled in the house when the newlyweds arrived home. Kate's poodle, whose home, until then, had only been Hovingham Hall, was no stranger now to the old, fading Persian rugs and the garden where the first flush of roses was over and Canterbury Bells and Phlox brightened the borders.

Inside, the faint dry scent of rose petals, the sweetish fragrance of Humea, the incense plant that had stood in the hall since Princess Victoria's day, the smell of beeswax polish still pervaded the house. But the heavy fumet of Marina's distinctive Turkish cigarettes had gone with the Princess, only to reappear when she visited Coppins in the future.

They started arranging their wedding presents on their first evening at home. They had been left, carefully stacked, in the music room which had always been the main salon as it was ideal for entertaining. Katharine had left a list at a London store and now she saw that their friends had given them many personal touches to help furnish their first home. From the staff at

Hovingham there were two engraved silver napkin rings – which would not have pleased Queen Mary who considered them middle class and only consented to use them during the war at Badminton when linen could not be laundered after every meal as in pre-war days. Two hand-painted tooth-brush mugs emblazoned with 'E' and 'K' went straight upstairs to their bathroom which adjoined the main bedroom where Princess Alexandra's gift, a large double bed, was already made up with the new linen presented by Worsley relatives. Six silver ash-trays and matchbox covers from Hovingham villagers were placed downstairs, along with a leather-topped coffee table from the Royal Household and other carefully chosen presents from royal relatives.

Like the wives who had successively left their touch on Hovingham Hall and given it such character, Coppins still retained the imprint of its previous royal occupants, despite the look and feel of the 'Sixties' its new mistress had given it. The bust of Edward VII, placed there by his daughter, Princess Victoria, remained in the entrance hall. Princess Marina's portrait still hung in the drawing room with Prince George's on the facing wall and in the late Duke's study all was still as he had left it that summer day in 1942, with his last note – faded now – 'Please do not move anything on this desk.'

It would not have been unnatural if, in her heart, Kate may have felt her mother-in-law's gesture in leaving the note there reflected morbid sentimentality. But all the Kents felt the same about the father they had lost so young. Eddie, in particular, was anxious to preserve all memories of his father in the house he had done so much to recreate, and even restored a rose bed beneath some windows because it had been there in Prince George's day.

Kate, herself, was far too sensitive and kind-hearted to change the established order which meant so much to all of them. In the kitchens, however, it was a different matter. They were eventually gutted and thoroughly modernized, although the portrait of Queen Victoria, first hung there in the 1870s by her lady-in-waiting, Jane Churchill, second owner of Coppins, remained in the staff room. In the garden, in the late autumn, Katharine and Eddie planted more roses – her favourite flower – including a hundred white and cream rose bushes from the Leicestershire grower whose blooms had decorated York Minster on their wedding day. There was also a new rose called 'Katharine Worsley' and some of these were duly planted at Coppins.

Their new notepaper, designed by Eddie, with its cypher of 'E' and 'K' entwined, gave added impetus to tackling the countless 'thank you' letters for wedding presents and good wishes which had flooded into Coppins and, whilst she could not possibly answer all of them herself, Kate wrote many personal notes to their friends and relatives.

Before long some of the small, thoughtful touches Lady Worsley had introduced at Hovingham began to be felt at Coppins as Kate felt more confident in her role. One of her ideas was to keep a small, enclosed rose garden for the family's private use and allow the staff the freedom of the rest of the grounds, as at Hovingham Hall.

By the autumn they knew that the nursery wing, last used by Eddie, Alex and Michael, would be needed again and, on Princess Marina's fifty-fifth birthday dinner in early December, celebrated at Coppins, they told her that she would soon be a grandmother. Meanwhile Eddie was still working at the War Office, driving up each day in the white Austin he used for London. Sometimes Kate went with him to lunch with friends or be dropped off at Kensington Palace to visit Princess Marina. She had a weekly hair appointment and liked to browse round the shops afterwards. But soon the distinctive blonde head and increasingly elegant clothes of the Duchess of Kent drew glances everywhere and she found, like all new royals, that every private moment was scrutinized.

It was nothing like the media attention presently endured by the Princess of Wales and the Duchess of York. But it was bad enough for the country-loving Yorkshire girl and visits to London grew more infrequent.

Kate had her first royal Christmas in 1961, at Sandringham House, the Queen's Norfolk home, not far from where she had been at school. Successive generations of royals have been fond of the rambling red-brick mansion since Prince Albert bought it for the then Prince of Wales, later Edward VII, hoping it would keep his son 'away from the gaming tables'. As heir to the throne and later as King, his father's original ploy succeeded. Edward grew increasingly attached to the country retreat he shared with Queen Alexandra, as their heirs were to do after them. Gregarious and much-travelled, the King loved returning 'home to Sandringham' which meant far more to him than any of his official residences. They had belonged to his predecessors but he and his Queen had created the Norfolk mansion rebuilt from an earlier house, set in magnificent grounds planted with rare trees and aglow in late spring with dense shrubberies of rhododendrons and azaleas.

They liked it in all seasons and filled 'the Big House' with myriad royal relatives from all over Europe. The Emperor of Germany and the Tsar of Russia, the King's nephews, and his niece, the Queen of Spain, visited Sandringham in the early days of the twentieth century, as did his brother-in-law, the King of Denmark. Fellow guests could be stage stars, writers, leaders of society or friends from the racing world. The King lived life to the full and enjoyed amusing company. The hospitality was lavish, fashionable and entertaining; the extravagant house parties of the Edwardian 'King's Set' were the talk of society. At Christmas he really became the country squire, surrounded by children and grandchildren with vast trees from the estate twinkling with light – following the custom brought to England by his father Prince Albert – and tables groaning with food.

Because of his bulky figure – he was nicknamed 'Tum-Tum' – Edward in later life rarely ate dinner with his guests because he could not bear the restriction of evening dress. So he dined from a tray in his room which must have been more comfortable for the portly King, who rejoined the family later in the drawing room.

His son George V who succeeded him was a very different character and when he and Queen Mary took over Sandringham, after the death of Queen Alexandra, the house surrendered to a more peaceful atmosphere. It had gradually lost its air of Edwardian gaiety during 'Mother dear's' long widowhood and now the ambience engendered by the quiet, shy and dignified George and Mary restored tranquillity to 'dear old Sandringham', as successive monarchs called it.

Some of the feeling of family Christmas at Sandringham – 'the place I love better than anywhere in the world' – was conveyed to a nation plunged into the depths of economic depression by George V in 1932 – Kate was nearly two – when he made the first of the now traditional broadcasts. It was a message of hope and cheer to those suffering hardship and unemployment and millions listened to his words which came from a cupboard under the stairs and were comforted by them.

George VI, father of the present Queen, echoed his father's feeling for Sandringham, saying: 'I want Lilibet and Philip to get to know it too ... I love the place.'

All newcomers to the Family get well briefed before embarking on their first Christmas 'at home' with the Queen because tradition plays so much a part of this royal holiday, as Kate learnt from her husband and mother-in-law.

The big family party assembles on the morning of Christmas Eve in good time for the present-giving ceremony in the evening – another custom introduced from the continent by the Prince Consort. Katharine had bought her presents, with some natural apprehension, helped by advice from Princess Alexandra who had warned her that the Royal Family did not expect lavish gifts. In a kind of inverted snobbery, they prefer unostentatious but appropriate gifts like the doormat Prince Charles gave his sister soon after she moved into Gatcombe Park.

They were ready, gaily wrapped in vivid paper, to be handed to a footman on arrival and conveyed to the white-covered tables beneath the giant Christmas tree, portioned off by bright ribbons for each member of the Family.

The new Duchess had been advised by her husband to write formal labels on each – with the recipient's full title – leaving any family nicknames, such as 'Pud' for Princess Alexandra or 'Lilibet' for the Queen, for the message inside the covers. This is not so much protocol but because presents are handed round by two footmen and three under-butlers who would, in the course of

The Duke and Duchess's wedding group taken in the ballroom of Hovingham Hall by the late Cecil Beaton. In the First World War it was used as a hospital ward and, in the Second World War, as Katharine remembers from her childhood, it was used to store gas masks.

The late Cecil Beaton's memorable picture of Katharine on her wedding day wearing John Cavanagh's classic dress, holding a bouquet of the white roses of York. It was the only photograph Princess Marina's old friend took of the bride alone because the Queen's press secretary, Richard Colville, insisted that Beaton took groups.

A portrait of the Duchess aged thirty-two (*above, left*), shortly before an official visit to the Gambia with the Duke for the Independence celebrations. The Queen was increasingly asking her Kent cousins to deputize for her on important engagements and was undoubtedly becoming aware of the young Duchess's potential, now fully realized.

Young parents with their two elder children (*above, right*) round the piano at Coppins, twenty-five years ago. The Earl of St Andrews was then four and his sister, Helen, two.

When the Duke and Duchess returned from army service abroad (*left*), they opened up Coppins, the family house, and settled down in Buckinghamshire. In due course, the children went to the local school and re-established friendships with their royal cousins. Prince Edward is the same age as Helen seen here with her mother and brother George.

In the garden at Coppins, the Duke and Duchess relax with their two children – soon there will be three. Katharine insisted on fulfilling military engagements in Hong Kong despite the fact that the Major-General was pregnant.

A happy family study of the Kents in 1975 at their then country home, Anmer Hall, on the Sandringham estate. But ahead lies tragedy for the Duke and Duchess with the loss, two years later, of the baby who would have increased the number of their children to four.

An appropriate greeting from the Duchess to a youngster at an international charity fair for children in London. At one of the stalls she bought some takeaway Chinese food of which she and her husband are fond.

Party time for the Duchess and a senior citizen. As always, she reaches out to make contact by gently stroking the pensioner's face – instantly conveying warmth and friendliness. 'I love old people,' she said once, 'and they need loving.'

(*Above left*) The Duchess with Chad Varah at the Samaritans Conference. She is very much a working patron; however, because of her increasing workload she no longer does a regular weekly duty at a Central London branch but is always alert for anyone who does need help of any kind. (*Above right*) Cancer Relief Macmillan Fund's Patron, HRH The Duchess of Kent, at the charity's Christmas Market, 1988.

Well-informed in military matters, the Duchess, once an army wife and herself Controller Commandant of the Women's Royal Army Corps, inspects men of the 4/7 Dragoon Guards.

Meeting the champion Boris Becker. The All-England Lawn Tennis Championships are always a feature of the Duchess's year and she was amused once to hear, up-country in India, a voice from the crowd calling, 'There's that lady from Wimbledon.'

When the Queen appointed the Duchess Controller Commandant of the WRAC with an honorary rank of Major-General, it meant she outranked her husband who was then a Major. Now a personal aide-de-camp to the Queen, he is Colonel of the Scots Guards and Colonel-in-Chief of the Royal Regiment of Fusiliers. But she still outranks him!

Dressing to go out on the town with her daughter, Helen, the Duchess forsakes the Romanov heirlooms and wears the sort of fake-but-fun jewellery Helen loves. Swinging from her ears are twin hearts and round her wrist a bracelet of more hearts. Only the string of pearls is loyally traditional.

On their silver wedding anniversary outside York House, St James's Palace. Photographer Jayne Fincher presented the Duchess with the basket of flowers which made an enchanting picture.

In one of the best pictures ever taken of the Duchess, the late Norman Parkinson – 'Parky' to the Royal Family – captured her luminous, fragile beauty emphasized by a filmy, ethereal ball gown.

An especially happy day for the
Duchess: the christening of her first
grandchild. The Princess of Wales was
a godmother and William Worsley, son
of Sir Marcus, a godfather,
appropriately 'linking the two families'.
The picture shows in the front row,
from the left: Miss Clare Stonor; the
Countess of St Andrews with the baby,
Lord Downpatrick; and the Princess of
Wales. In the back row (from left): Hon
Tim Knatchbull; Count Nicholas
Czapary: the Earl of St Andrews and
William Worsley.

The Duchess with the Prince of Wales
at a formal engagement (*below, left*). Of
all the Royal Family she perhaps best
understands his need for meditation
and solitude to restore the serenity that
stressful public life so often lacks.

Looking happy and relaxed in a
stunning white off-the-shoulder dress
(*below, right*) and long chandelier
earrings, the Duchess attends a charity
premiere in London.

A painting of HRH The Duchess of Kent by Leonard Boden RP, FRSA. The painting hangs in Glaziers' Hall, London Bridge. Mr Boden is an experienced royal portraitist, whose past sitters have included HM The Queen, HRH The Prince of Wales and the Duke of Edinburgh.

duty, naturally see the labels. Someone did read the inside labels after one Christmas at Windsor and the amusing and affectionate little messages were published in a Sunday paper.

The Queen likes masses of relatives around but when the Family increased significantly in the 'baby boom' of the Sixties, she moved the Christmas venue to Windsor Castle where there was more room. Recently, while the Castle is undergoing structural repairs, the celebrations have once again been held at Sandringham with the Kent family, which has also grown considerably, at nearby Anmer Hall. This country home, lent to them by the Queen, has been recently vacated for one they have bought nearer London. When anyone visits one of her homes for the first time the Queen likes to show them round herself and, that first Christmas at Sandringham, she introduced Kate to some Edwardian nostalgia. In the white, blue and gold drawing room it is particularly prevalent, dominated by a portrait of Queen Alexandra and her fabulous collection of Fabergé animals; three hundred of them carved in semi-precious stones decorate the room. Generations of royal children have loved them, especially the trumpeting elephants in rock crystal and jade and a dormouse with bright eyes of small diamonds and fine gold whiskers. Queen Alexandra herself adored the dogs, some modelled on her own – poodles, bulldogs, collies, dachshunds, and her favourite pekinese.

Also modelled by Carl Fabergé was the King's dog Caesar (who walked behind his coffin ahead of Kings, Emperors and Princes and had his own footman). So fascinated were Edward and his Queen with the work of the St Petersburg jeweller and goldsmith that they asked him to send modellers to Sandringham to copy their farm animals – shire horses, hens, ducks, even pigs. Persimmon, the royal Derby winner cast in silver and jewels, a great favourite of Elizabeth II, was also modelled.

Outside, in the gardens, guests walking off their Christmas meals may find themselves strolling past the graves of Queen Alexandra's beloved dogs which have now been joined by those of the Queen.

On Christmas morning everyone goes to church including members of the staff – all except the chefs and kitchen workers who are busy producing turkey and plum pudding for the two sittings: royal and staff dining rooms. The menus are similar except the first course; the staff begin with mushroom or tomato soup – the Royal Family with lobster and asparagus bisque. After lunch everyone watches the Queen's television appearance and in the evening comes another candlelit meal, followed by family games. On Boxing Day there is a pheasant shoot followed, in the evening after dinner, with a cinema show – always a film suitable for children and to which the staff, also, are invited. 'It never varies – we'd all hate it if it did,' said the Duke who had spent many Christmases of his life with his cousins.

Kate, three months pregnant, may have thought nostalgically of her mother presiding over the festival at the Hall. It was the first time in her life she had been away from Hovingham at Christmas. She felt unwell during the church service on Christmas Day and had to leave before the end, escorted by a young Prince Charles. The Queen, understanding and sympathetic, with her own third baby only two years old, suggested tactfully that afternoon that, perhaps, it was time to make Kate's news public. The next day it was announced from Coppins that she was expecting a baby in the early summer.

Kate went up to Hovingham in February to celebrate her twenty-ninth birthday with her parents but, apart from visits to family and friends, she and Eddie lived very quietly at Coppins until the baby arrived.

Alexandra, enchanted at the prospect of becoming an aunt, brought back baby clothes and presents from all her overseas engagements that year and remembers an excited telephone call from her mother one June day. 'Come at once,' said the deep, husky voice of Princess Marina who had already installed herself at Coppins with Sir William and Lady Worsley. 'Kate is starting to have her baby. And she needs all her family with her.'

Bubbling with excitement and already emotional, Marina showed that day how completely Kate had won her over. Her natural reticence had fallen away in face of her growing affection for her daughter-in-law. The Worsleys and Kents celebrated on 26 June 1962, like a totally integrated family who had known each other all their lives. This achievement from comparative strangers was entirely due to the gentle, happy young woman who, in becoming a wife and mother, was the link between them.

The cause of all the jubilation was the six pounds, four ounces, Earl of St Andrews, born tenth in line to the throne. He was also the first male child in the direct line to be born without the title 'Prince'. King George V, his great-grandfather, had decreed in 1917 that the royal title should end after the grandchildren of the Sovereign.

Technically, he was a commoner but that did not worry his deeply contented parents or the mothers of Iver village who had the happy inspiration of each sending the most beautiful rose from her garden to make a very personal bouquet of June roses for Katharine on the birth of her son.

Setting a new fashion, to be followed in later years by Prince Andrew, the Duke who was a keen amateur photographer himself took the first pictures of his Duchess and her child, soon after his birth. Lord Snowdon had, in fact, taken the pictures of his first child, Lord Linley, a few months earlier but he was a professional photographer and not a member of the Royal Family.

When Eddie had downed a celebratory glass of champagne with the family, he drafted the announcement from Coppins: 'Her Royal Highness the Duchess of Kent was safely delivered of a son. Both the Duchess and her child are well.' From Buckingham Palace both the Queen and Prince Philip, who two years before had started their 'second family' with the birth of Prince Andrew, personally telephoned Coppins to speak to Princess Marina and Edward in turn.

Then, a few days later, knowing of the great interest in the new arrival, Kate suggested to Nanny Mary McPherson that she wheel the baby to the gates of Coppins so that the small crowd of villagers could have a glimpse of him.

For his christening in September most of the Royal Family forsook the normally sacrosanct holiday at Balmoral to be present in the music room at Buckingham Palace when the blond, blue-eyed infant was given the name of George (after his great-grandfather George V and his grandfather, the late Duke of Kent). He was also named Philip after his godfather, the Duke of Edinburgh, and Nicholas after his other great-grandfather, Prince Nicholas of Greece. At his christening in Buckingham Palace, the usual ritual of all royal babies was followed: the gold lily font travelled from Windsor, as did the fragile Honiton lace christening robe used by Queen Victoria's children. It was shaken from the black tissue paper in which it is always kept and carefully put on baby George by nanny Mary, who was terrified it would tear.

Later that year, leaving 'Georgie' in the capable hands of his nurse, the Duke and Duchess flew to Uganda where they were to represent the Queen at the Independence ceremonies – their first important public engagement together. For Katharine it was also her first experience of a formal overseas trip as a royal Duchess and, although she felt excited, she was also understandably nervous.

The Queen helped her considerably as she does with all fledgling royals before they 'fly' on their own. She and her dresser Margaret ('Bobo') MacDonald, by then an old hand at choosing clothes suitable for all climates, advised on the wardrobe she would need for the State Opening of Parliament, ceremonial drives and garden parties, visits to hospitals and schools – all the different duties a royal visit entails. 'It will be hot,' they warned.

John Cavanagh, who had made her wedding dress, guided her in the elegant way she has dressed ever since, with a wardrobe of simple, exquisitely cut clothes in the clear, bright colours the Duchess likes. Belinda Belville who had made her bridesmaids' dresses also contributed to the wardrobe for the tour which, in blazing equatorial heat, was counted an undoubted success and made the Queen aware of the potential, now fully realized, of Kate Kent.

At the end there was the personal highlight of a weekend off, spent in the Queen Elizabeth National Park in Kenya, where Kate was enchanted by 'five elephants having their breakfast outside our bedroom windows'. That short weekend was the prelude to another stage in the Duchess's life: her overseas postings, with her husband, as an 'army wife' which took her first to the Far East and then to Germany.

8

Army Wife

Privacy is a rare luxury in a royal marriage. Even in the closed world of home there is someone nearby keeping a watchful eye – if only for security reasons. However kind and welcoming the loyal, long-serving staff at Coppins had been to their new mistress, there had been all too few occasions when the newly-married couple had been alone for any length of time.

For the born-royals, it is a way of life, totally accepted. For those who marry into 'the Family', it sometimes takes time to adjust – as the Princess of Wales and the Duchess of York have found – and become accustomed to the constant beam of the spotlight, whether public or domestic. For a junior member public exposure can, at first, appear mercifully intermittent. But those fitful rays can swiftly flare into a relentless glare as with Marina Ogilvy's all too public clash with her parents, Princess Alexandra and Sir Angus Ogilvy. It was an unfortunate affair which sent shudders through the Royal Family and the Kents, normally reticent in their private lives, went even further into their shell.

But back in 1962, Princess Alexandra's happy and successful marriage to Angus was still a few months away and the advent of Marina, their second child, still further on the horizon. For Kate, the year of her first son's birth, was a welcome respite, broken only by a few royal duties which gave her a chance to learn the ropes in her own time.

Edward's posting overseas pleased the Queen, whose own memories of an idyllic spell in Malta, as a navy wife, when her husband's ship was based there, are among the happiest of her early married life. She and the rest of the family hoped it would be the same for Eddie and Kate.

He departed for Hong Kong in mid-November ahead of his family, to take up his duties as second-in-command of 'C' Squadron of the Royal Scots Greys at their Sek Kong base. Kate was scheduled to join him two weeks later after she had closed up Coppins for eighteen months. She left the house, with baby George and Mary McPherson, reasonably early for their flight. But, as a pea-soup fog descended, the driver lost his way to Stanstead airport and even the ever-calm Scots girl began to get panicky as it became clear they were going to miss the plane. Telephone calls eventually established that the flight had been postponed because of the weather and at Kensington Palace Princess Marina was roused at midnight by the travellers, seeking beds and hot, comforting drinks.

They set off again next day for a long, tiring journey on a packed Britannia troop charter aircraft – a very different flight from the Britannia, royally-fitted, that had taken Kate and Eddie to Uganda only a few weeks before. Now, as an army wife and the first member of the Royal Family to travel on a 'women and children' flight, she sat in the forward section reserved for mothers with young babies. She shared the job of changing nappies with Mary and fed George in the curtained-off 'babies' room' with brief interludes when they touched down at Istanbul and Bombay.

As others cried around him, George – always an amiable child – proved a model traveller and remained good-humoured throughout. Perhaps, because of the shared duties, he had more than his quota of fun-time and cuddling. However, the atmosphere in the plane plus the usual indifferent food, the more or less constant crying of one or other of the infants and the antics of the bored older children during a two-day journey did not make it a relaxing trip.

The weary wives raised a small cheer as Hong Kong drew near. They flew low over the emerald sea, streaked with boats of every description from ocean liners and ferries to small sampan junks. Behind the harbour rose the jagged roofs and towers of the mass of concrete that has taken the place of the more picturesque masts of clipper ships as landmarks of the busiest and richest port in the Far East.

The Duke was waiting at the airport with other husbands, delighted to see his wife and baby looking so fresh and beautiful – a minor miracle which had been achieved in the cramped washroom on the plane. He drove them in his small Ford to Barbecue Gardens in the Castle Peak district of the Kowloon mainland. There, on the upper floor of a white concrete army house, was their home in Hong Kong.

A bigger contrast to Kensington Palace where they had stayed on their last night in Britain could not be imagined. But, like any woman in a new home, Kate ran excitedly from room to room as though the flat with three small bedrooms, living room, kitchen and bathroom was the most ideal home in the world. Then she took in the view from the small terrace which looked over other people's back gardens to the shining but distinctly crowded sea.

There is always something to look at in Hong Kong which the Kents found after a few days in their new home as their windows faced the sea looking over towards the harbour. Backwards and forwards across the waterway between Tsim Sha Tsui and Central – old Victoria on Hong Kong island – ply the green and white ferries which, like everyone who lives in the colony, Kate got to know well. When she returned to Hong Kong on an official visit she was delighted to see them again, crossing as usual, hundreds of times a day. Somehow their romantic names – Lone Star, Twinkling Stars, Morning Star, Celestial, Northern, Shining, Day, Silver and Meridian – enhance a commuter's everyday journey as the Duchess found on trips to Victoria several times a month.

As their flat was so small, compared to Coppins, it was as well Kate and Mary – whose last job had been as nursemaid to the factor's family at Balmoral – got on so well for, certainly by royal standards, their quarters were cramped. But, on the ground floor, lived Captain Simon Cox and his wife who gladly gave up one of their bedrooms for Nanny and George if the Kents had anyone to stay. And outside the kitchen window was a small service balcony where the Chinese amah, who came in daily, hung George's nappies and small baby clothes.

Kate already knew most of the wives of Eddie's brother officers and, with ready-made friends, plunged into the bright new world that awaited her on the small, hilly granite island the Chinese call 'Incense Port', or 'Fragrant Harbour'. Despite the inevitable stepladder of social hierarchy endemic in small communities, the busy and enjoyable life suited her and she blossomed happily in 'the Come-and-Go Island' – so called because of its fluctuating population.

The joy of being stationed there was that it was possible to be both a tourist and a resident, a holiday-maker and 'old Hong Kong hand' even after only a few weeks. Kate got to know only too well the smell once described as 'oily, laced with duck mess and gasoline'. Tourists in the de luxe hotels rarely find in their nostrils this pungent mix that is so peculiarly Hong Kong. She also knew the herby scent of the grass when she and Eddie walked in the hills at weekends, where lady-slipper orchids hid in the hollows and hibiscus and camellias bloomed, wild and glorious.

Like others had done before them, they gazed down in the late evening from Victoria Peak to see Hong Kong spread out below them, its lights scintillating like hundreds of precious stones and all around them the fragrance of jasmine and daphne clustered beneath banks of rhododendrons and azaleas in the spring.

A thoughtful cleric who visited Hong Kong in the 1840s, at the height of its early trading prosperity, would not have had the opportunity to be enchanted by the wonder of thousands of twinkling lights. For electricity was yet to come. Instead he was filled with patriotic complacency: 'I sometimes imagine Britannia standing on the Peak and looking down with an emotion of pride upon the great Babylon which her sons have built,' wrote the Reverend James Legge.

Kate and Eddie got to know the sounds of Hong Kong; the wooden shoes clattering on pavements, a constant click of dice as ancient maj-jong – played in China since the Song dynasty – triumphed over the challenge of the electronic computer games which tourists take home. There was the almost constant hooting of bumper-to-bumper traffic at rush hour in and around the city. In the Chinese New Year, when most sensible Europeans wear ear plugs, the sounds were intensified hugely as the deafening noise of firecrackers exploded endlessly during the forty-eight hours the law allows them. During it Chinese greet friends and acquaintances with their equivalent of 'Happy New Year'. These money-conscious men and women say instead: 'Respectfully hope you get rich'.

The Kents went regularly to Chinese operas and to concerts of the Hong Kong Philharmonic. They were keen movie-goers too, preferring to view in their local cinema when a film of Princess Alexandra's engagement to the Hon Angus Ogilvy arrived in the Colony and they were offered a private view. They sailed, played tennis and water skied. Eddie played polo and they both watched cricket. Kate rode as much as she could, even entering one of the army ponies for a gymkana when she repeated her childhood feat of jumping through a blazing hoop. There were picnics, regattas, balls and racing at Happy Valley.

When Eddie was away on training exercises with his Squadron, Kate explored Hong Kong with friends. They saw all the usual sights like the crescent graves, some with tall brown urns of family ashes, in the Chinese Cemetery and the spot where one hundred women were forced to stamp on a hill until they made, eventually and after much hardship, a flat plain. As all visitors to the Colony do, they visited the monastery of Po Lin, up in the hills, with the dimly-lit Man Mo temple, scented with incense. In the walled village of Kat Hing Wai at Kam Tim they watched as old women of the Tang clan smoked traditional pipes and posed for visitors' cameras.

Meanwhile 'Georgie' was growing up fast, as Kate wrote home to his two grandmothers, Princess Marina and Lady Worsley. He was crawling everywhere, so speedy on his knees that the Chinese amah called him 'the little one with the winged knees'. Kate used to take him to the nearby park in his pram most afternoons, casual, in cotton dress and coolie sandals, her hair often tied back in a pony-tail. Beneath the trees the two blonde heads were very close together as she played with him, forming early the bond between them that has grown closer with the years. His first birthday, remembered with presents and cards from all the royal and Worsley relatives, was memorable in family annals because it coincided with the Taipo Dragon Festival, in honour of the moon, which the Chinese considered a particularly favourable omen for the little one. Eddie entered a twenty-six man army crew of British and Ghurkas for the Dragon boat race, one of the highlights of the celebrations.

But, as the drums pounded to the rhythm of the oars, their boat with its colourful red and gold dragon head and tail began to sink. The crew had to tow it over the finishing line, swimming alongside to the intense amusement of the skipper's wife, who filmed it from an accompanying speedboat. 'The Duchess was laughing so much she could hardly hold the camera,' said one of her friends.

A favourite expedition was to dine alone or with friends in one of the floating houseboat restaurants at the fishing town of Aberdeen. There, by the many moored junks, there are always groups of boat-women, distinctive with their straw hats, black trousers and aprons, waiting to row prospective diners out to the restaurants. They normally wait for the return journey, enjoying by way of an accepted bonus whatever is left of the huge, sumptuous meal, usually too much for the diners.

Kate and Eddie grew to love Chinese cooking as organizers of a Christmas fair in London discovered many years later when she bought four takeaway meals to take home. 'We shall enjoy this,' she said, explaining they had learnt to eat Chinese in Hong Kong.

Noël Coward went to visit them during a trip to the Far East and wrote in his diary: 'A really enchanting evening with Prince Eddie and Kathy who live in an ordinary officer's issue flatlet in the New Territories ... merry as grigs and having a lovely time untrammelled by royal pomposity. They really are a sweet couple and it is a pleasure to see two people so entirely happy with each other. I also saw George who is thirteen months and blond and pink and smiling.'

The Kents had by now got used, when they went into Victoria, to hearing the noonday salute fired by a Hotchkiss three pounder gun, made in 1901 at the start of great-great-grandfather Edward VIII's reign, which roared from the quayside each day. It was difficult to hear it without thinking, as many people do, of Coward's catchy song: 'Mad Dogs and Englishmen' ...

> 'In Hong Kong
> they strike a gong
> and fire off a mid-day gun
> to reprimand each inmate
> who's late ...'

In April 1963, as Hong Kong simmered in blazing temperatures, they flew home, leaving George with Mary McPherson, for the wedding of Alex and Angus. They arrived early so that the two sisters-in-law could go together to John Cavanagh's salon for all the excitement of the final fitting – a nostalgic experience for Kate bringing back, as it did, memories of the dress he had made for her own wedding two years before. The gleaming silk of the bridal gown was, like Kate's, specially ordered from France and its hue of warm magnolia complimented a length of old Valenciennes lace which Princess Marina had worn at her own wedding. It was part of the bridal ensemble of Alex's grandmother, Princess Nicholas of Greece, and with it she had worn the fabulous pink diamond of Catherine the Great of Russia, a traditional part of the wedding for all Romanov brides.

Cavanagh had designed a sweeping court train for Alexandra, edged by a wide band of the exquisite lace which was worn in place of a veil, held by a narrow diamond tiara. Kata was able to offer some advice on how to cope with the twenty-one feet of material which would be anchored only by the tiara. 'Don't do what I did and get it caught up,' she said. 'That was almost disaster.'

A huge influx of foreign royals, amongst many other relatives,

arrived in London for the wedding, much to Marina's joy, for
she wanted Katharine to meet those she may not have encountered
at her own wedding. 'There are rather a lot of them,' she mur-
mured as she reeled off a string of names straight out of the
Almanac de Gotha: The King of Norway, the Queen of Greece,
the Queen of Denmark, Queen Victoria-Eugenie of Spain, Queen
Helen of Romania, the Crown Prince of Greece, the Crown Prince
of Norway, Princess Irene of Greece, Princess Anne-Marie of
Denmark, Princess Irene of the Netherlands, Princess Margriet
of the Netherlands, the Princess Hohenlohe-Langenburg, the
Prince and Princess of the Asturias, the Margrave and Margravine
of Baden, Prince and Princess George of Hanover, the Duchess
of Aosta, the Prince and Princess of Hesse and the Rhine, Prince
Ludwig of Baden, Princess Beatrix of Hohenlohe-Langenburg,
Prince Ruprecht of Hohenlohe-Langenburg, Prince and Princess
Frederick Windisch-Graelz and Princess Clarissa of Hesse.

It could not have been easy for Kate to distinguish one from
the other in this formidable assembly all descended from Queen
Victoria let alone remember their names. She was, after all, a
comparative newcomer to the enormous European family of
royals. 'How great-great-grandmamma would have loved it,' said
the Queen to Prince Philip, as they all descended on Windsor
Castle. In fact the Queen was particularly pleased to meet up with
so many relatives, many of whom she had been unable to ask to
her own wedding because it was still so near to the war – and
they were German.

Every guest suite in the Castle was pressed into service and a
unique bus tour organized for the following day during which
the Queen and her husband conducted their guests around the
local sights of Windsor, including the royal mausoleum at Frogmore where Queen Victoria and Prince Albert are interred.

To entertain them still further and celebrate her cousin's
wedding, the Queen threw a magnificent ball for two thousand
guests – some say the most lavish since Edward VII's day. The
Waterloo Chamber, which commemorates Britain's victory over
the French, looked its finest with the oil paintings wreathed in
flowers and more blooms in the large gold candelabra. Standing

by unobtrusively with watering cans at the ready was a team of gardeners ready to administer first aid if the flowers showed signs of wilting.

Kate had attended at least one royal ball since she had known Eddie – the one given by the Queen to welcome home Princess Alexandra from her first solo Far Eastern tour – before their engagement. But this was even more glamorous with its setting of the thousand-year-old floodlit castle and the excitement of meeting so many new royal faces. From a balcony overlooking the scene Prince Charles and Princess Anne, still only fifteen and thirteen, waved to people they knew well and the heir to the throne recorded the event, for family consumption, with his mother's cine camera.

Joe Loss's band struck up the opening number and Angus Ogilvy, after an encouraging nod from the Queen, led his bride on to the floor, limping slightly because of a leg injury after a recent motor crash which had alarmed the Royal Family. After some sedate numbers the band swung into the twist, the 'in' dance of that year and some of Europe's most distinguished men and women threw themselves into the spirit of the lively number led by the Queen and Prince Philip, much to the amusement of their teenage offspring who were doing their own version above.

A particularly acute observer of the scene was that old friend of the Kents', Noël Coward, who could have given a new look to a Ruritanian musical with the antics of these 'swinging Sixties' royals.

Later, as a compliment to the Scottish bridegroom, son of the Earl and Countess of Airlie, pipers of the Scots Guards – his old regiment – played for the Highland dancing which all the royals, foreign or British, joined in enthusiastically.

The Kent family (Min, Eddie, Kate, Alex and Maow) drove back to London where they were all staying in Marina's Kensington Palace apartment.

During the ceremony, Kate, who was sitting with her mother-in-law and Michael in the family seats in Westminster Abbey, felt some nostalgia for her own wedding which, although only two years ago, seemed much further away. The Duke of Kent, tall and surprisingly assured as he had confessed to feeling nervous earlier, escorted his sister down the aisle and gave her away to Angus Ogilvy.

He and Kate were moved to hear another link with their own wedding – the strains of Widor's Toccata in F which both they and the Ogilvys had chosen for their wedding march. Later, after a reception at St James's Palace, the bride and bridegroom sped to London airport, honeymoon-bound, in Princess Marina's Rolls. It was suitably decorated with a tartan ribbon and a baby's shoe – organized by Eddie Kent, Charles Wales and their cousin Juan Carlos, now King of Spain.

Back in Hong Kong in the muggy heat of early autumn, Kate knew she was pregnant again and a letter from Alexandra confirmed that she was also. But, as it turned out, they were not the only ones in the family who were expecting babies. At the Christmas get-together of the Royal Family at Sandringham there were even more prospective babes to celebrate. 'To all the small strangers we know are present,' quipped the Duke of Edinburgh, raising his glass in a toast full of uncharacteristic schmaltz.

It was indeed a unique family occasion, for not since the four daughters of George III had all been expecting at the same time had there been such a prolific royal baby boom.

The mothers-to-be were the Queen, Princess Margaret, the Duchess of Kent and Princess Alexandra whose babies – born so close together – grew up as a quartet who were rarely separated during the school holidays of their childhood.

Despite their pregnancies the outdoor life of Sandringham continued as usual, enjoyed by one and all. 'The whole family', said Mabel Anderson, nanny to the Queen's children and later Princess Anne's, 'goes out in weather most would think was mad.' The four royal women joined the guns as usual for picnic lunches, laughing together because their normal agility at retrieving pheasants was somewhat impaired.

The Kents went home to Coppins to celebrate the New Year with Princess Marina in the old Russian style. Nineteen sixty three had been a happy and fulfilling family year but events outside had made it a difficult twelve months for others. Among the big news stories was the saga of Princess Marina's friend John Profumo who was involved in a 'call-girl' scandal that rocked Harold Macmillan's Tory government and contributed to its fall. And an audacious gang perpetrated 'The Great Train Robbery' making off with well over a million pounds. As the year drew to its end, a shocked world learnt that President John Kennedy had been assassinated in Dallas, Texas.

In her personal life Kate found she was sailing through this second pregnancy, even more happy and serene than she had been when George was expected. She decided to join Eddie in St Moritz for the Army Ski Championships in January, which she had not done before in case she slipped in the snow.

Before flying home for Christmas they had said a regretful farewell to Hong Kong and the small flat in which they had been so happy. Now they were about to begin a tour of duty in Germany where the regiment would be based for the next two years. Ahead lay another home and another chapter in Kate's early married life.

9

Sunshine and Shadow

Katharine was still taking prospective motherhood naturally and easily with the help of the relaxation classes she attended at a special clinic. Having three other prospective mums in the family was almost like sharing their pregnancies and cousins and sisters-in-law kept in touch with each other's progress, just as they have always taken a special interest in the four royal children who arrived so close together and have been friends ever since.

Forsaking Hovingham for her thirty-first birthday celebrations that year, Kate went instead to Fallingbostel where the Scots Greys were stationed to spend the day with Eddie and inspect the house that would be their home in the immediate future. After that there was little time before the first of the expected family babies arrived: James Ogilvy, son of Alexandra and Angus Ogilvy, born in the thirteenth hour of 29 February 1964, was a nine pounds, six ounces Leap Year baby who, henceforth, would only have an official birthday every four years. Kate was one of the first visitors to see her godson in the Ogilvys' home, Thatched House Lodge in Richmond Park, Surrey, and helped the new parents toast the future of James, then thirteenth in succession to the throne after his cousin George Kent.

The next baby to arrive was Prince Edward, youngest son of the Queen and the Duke of Edinburgh, on 10 March, and the Queen, who had become increasingly fond of Kate, asked her to be his godmother. After that it was the turn of the Kents to add to their family with a daughter, Lady Helen Windsor, on 29 April. Kate had hoped to be present at the Buckingham Palace christening of Prince Edward. But his future playmate was on her way and she barely had time to alert Eddie in Germany before she went into labour.

Princess Marina was already at Coppins, after standing in for her daughter-in-law at the christening; anxious, as always, to share her family's important events. She greeted Eddie when he arrived, after a hasty plane journey, with a stiff drink and the news that the birth was imminent.

The third of the royal quartet was a bouncing baby of seven pounds, eight ounces – another blonde like her mother and brother. 'We are delighted with my first granddaughter,' Princess Marina wrote to her sister Princess Olga, 'especially as Katharine longed for a girl.'

Helen, named after her beautiful Romanov great-grandmother, the Grand Duchess Helen Vladimirovna of Russia, later Princess Nicholas of Greece, was born just three days before her cousin and future great friend, Lady Sarah Armstrong-Jones, daughter of Princess Margaret and Lord Snowdon.

The Queen, delighted with the latest additions to her family which meant that Edward would have three cousins of the same age as companions, threw a luncheon party at Windsor Castle for Helen's christening on 6 June, two days before her parents' third wedding anniversary. Most of the Royal Family and the Worsley family, including her godparents Princess Margaret and Angus Ogilvy, attended the ceremony in the private chapel at Windsor. Following custom the infant was sprinkled with holy water from the River Jordan from the gold lily font, wearing the Honiton lace christening robe – which was having a busy year. Treated with reverence and care as befitted its long history, it was shaken out of its black tissue paper and then gently replaced until the next royal baby's baptism. Kate and Eddie's daughter was christened Helen Marina Lucy – the last a Brunner family name; Katharine, herself, has it because it was the name of her maternal grandmother who married Sir John Brunner, son of the Victorian philanthropist.

Within a few weeks Coppins was again closed and Kate and Mary McPherson, this time with two young children, flew to Hanover to resume life on a British army base. By a quirk of fate their new home – a standard 'married accommodation' detached house in Quebec Avenue – was not far from where Eddie's Hanoverian ancestors had once lived and ruled. From the small kingdom of Hanover, the future George I set off to claim the British throne at the start of the Hanoverian dynasty.

He was the Protestant descendant of Elizabeth Stuart, 'the Winter Queen' of Bohemia, daughter of King James I, who married the Elector Palatine of the Rhine. Their daughter, the Electress Sophia, was sister of Prince Rupert of the Rhine, the dashing Cavalier general who fought for his uncle King Charles I against the Roundheads. Their leader was Oliver Cromwell, Lord Protector of England and the Duchess of Kent's ancestor.

Fascinated as she may well have been by the coincidence, Kate had more prosaic matters on her mind as she settled into her new home. She could not do much about the furniture, which had been supplied more for its hard-wearing qualities than beauty or elegance. But new lamps, cushions and other individual touches made their latest home more their own. The house had one more bedroom than their flat in Hong Kong which was a decided plus but the garden was tiny – a dismal change from the spacious grounds of Coppins where toddler George had safely played and baby Helen snoozed in her pram.

Kate was soon absorbed again in army life; renewing friendships made in Hong Kong with other wives of the regiment who treated her in a relaxed friendly fashion as one of themselves. The only difference was that if a prize had to be presented in the normal course of regimental life, it tended to be the Duchess of Kent and not the CO's wife who did the honours. But it was no more than she would have done at home in Hovingham as the daughter of the squire at local events. She had yet to realize that, later on, as a full-time working royal, life would not be so carefree. There would be a gulf around her that separated her from everyone else. Her life would be lived 'behind a glass curtain', as Marion Crawford, governess to Princesses Elizabeth and Margaret, once described it. As yet it was not apparent, but in the years to come the constraints of her position and the constant exposure in public life would bring private spasms of frustration and take their toll of the Duchess's naturally happy serenity.

With their young family, she and Eddie explored their corner of Germany in his E-type Jaguar. Not far away lived first cousin Hans Veit of Toerring, nine months younger than Eddie, whom he had known all his life. Hans's mother had been Countess Toerring, the former Princess Elizabeth ('Woolly'), sister of Princess Marina, who had died in 1955. The Duke of Edinburgh's nephew, Prince Kraft of Hohenlohe, who they had last seen at Alexandra's wedding, was another relative with whom they spent happy, relaxed weekends.

These two young men were part of the complex network that formed a necklace of royal relatives around Europe before the First World War. At the beginning of the century, when Eddie's parents George and Marina were born, this exclusive circle of royals monopolized both society and the politics of the day, intermarrying and creating even more intricate and powerful alliances.

After the war this power waned; monarchies were toppled, the most significant being the Russian throne and the Imperial family, from which Marina was directly descended through her mother Princess Nicholas of Greece, before her marriage a Grand Duchess and niece of Tsar Alexander III.

But several strong dynasties remained, among them the thrones of Scandinavia, the Netherlands and Belgium and it was an alliance with such another royal family that Marina had wanted for her children.

During his time in Germany, as regimental adjutant, the Duke – now turning out to be a fine soldier – was working hard for his staff college exam and he and Kate often spent evenings going over likely questions and answers. She found herself becoming well-informed in military matters which helped her cope more realistically when the Queen appointed her Controller Commandant of the Women's Royal Army Corps.

Once again the Duchess had pram-pushing afternoons with her two children, free to be an ordinary wife and mother. 'They were happy days,' she said recently to an army wife who had been in Germany at the same time. From time to time the Queen asked the Kents to help out in the family team – like flying to Africa in February 1965 for the Independence celebrations in Gambia. It was eight years since the country had seen a member of the Queen's family and they were given an enthusiastic welcome by its 320,000 people.

At the end of the two years, Kate returned to Coppins to open up the house for permanent occupation whilst her husband 'lived in' at an army college where he was doing a three-month military science course.

Staff was hard to come by at first and Kate and Mary coped alone for the first few months with occasional help from women in Iver village. The summer of 1966 – when the bank rate was raised to seven per cent and England beat Germany at football to win the World Cup for the first time – was a halcyon few months for the Kents. The old Coppins nurseries were freshly painted and occupied again and the rose garden Kate and Eddie had planted and set aside for the family was at its most beautiful.

The children's personalities were emerging and they were a complete contrast to one another. George, four in June, was good-natured but with a sensitive, reserved streak. Already he was showing the brightness that would take him along a scholastic path. Helen, the two-year-old toddler, was blonde and bouncy as she continued to be; pushy and assertive but with her mother's kind heart.

Their parents contrived to bring them up very normally, inviting local children to play at Coppins and, in due course, they went, at first, to neighbourhood schools. Always there was close contact with their royal cousins and one of the first parties Kate gave was a nursery one when the Queen brought Prince Andrew, six, and Prince Edward, two – Kate's godson – over to tea.

Princess Alexandra's second child, a daughter, was born on 31 July and given the truly regal names of Marina Victoria (after her great-great-great-grandmother) and Alexandra after her mother and her great-great-grandmother, the Consort of Edward VII. These illustrious royal ladies would not have cared for the behaviour of the baby named after them when she grew up. By telling the story of a dispute with her parents to a tabloid newspaper, Marina – by then pregnant by the boyfriend whom she later married – broke all the rules of family loyalty, regal or otherwise.

She certainly had a marvellous start and a right royal welcome into the world. Prince Charles and Princess Margaret were godparents, the King and Queen of Thailand visited her as an infant, King Constantine of Greece gave a dinner party in honour of her christening where, as usual with royal babies, she wore the family christening robe. Most of the Royal Family were present and the ceremony was conducted by the Archbishop of Canterbury.

That summer of her niece's birth, Kate spent a happy holiday at Hovingham with her children installed in her old nursery where the familiar toy London bus, innumerable teddy bears and other toys were waiting for a new generation.

Back home it became apparent that 'Georgie' was ready for school. Very much like the Worsleys in appearance, he had obviously inherited his brains from both sides of the family. Kate's brothers were all Oxford graduates and Queen Mary always said Prince George, his grandfather and namesake, was the clever one of her brood. They enrolled him in the village school where he showed a talent for painting and music and movement classes. His mother gave him his first riding lessons on a pony called Lucifer and helped him practise the piano at which he showed promise, hopefully inheriting the family passion for music.

Princess Marina smiled nostalgically when she heard Georgie's first efforts. 'Just like his grandfather,' she said, recalling how her husband – as 'Chips' Channon put it – used to 'idly strum Debussy' on his Ibeck baby grand or the Steinway in the music room.

Kate gradually began to take on some public duties. She was invited to become Chancellor of Leeds University and accepted gladly, feeling it right that one of her first royal tasks should be a Yorkshire one. But her public engagements remained low-key, as Princess Marina was still *the* Duchess of Kent in the eyes of the public and always would be in her lifetime. Her daughter-in-law wanted to avoid any intrusion, however unintentional, into the perimeter of her royal duties.

Princess Marina, as Commandant of the Women's Royal Naval Service, had been a glamorous incentive to recruitment during the war. 'Every time her photograph appeared in uniform there was a rush to join up,' said Dame Vera Laughton Matthews, then director of the WRNS. The Queen felt Katharine could do the same for the Women's Royal Army Corps and her new appointment, carrying the honorary rank of Major General, meant that his wife now outranked the Duke who was then a Major. Royal couturier Norman Hartnell designed her dark green uniform which he made two inches above regulation length – 'long skirts are ageing', he always used to say. The Duchess felt this slight deviation from regulations was one royal perk of which she should take advantage.

In 1967 the Queen asked her cousins to represent her at the Coronation of the new ruler of Tonga, Taufa hau Tupon IV – an opportunity to visit the South Seas and enjoy the legendary hospitality of the Tongans. When the Queen visited the country for the first time during her Coronation Tour of the Commonwealth, Queen Salote – an immense lady who had scored an enormous success with the London crowds when travelling in the Coronation procession – was waiting to greet the Queen in one of her proudest possessions – the London taxi she had ordered during her visit to Britain during the Coronation in 1953.

The Queen warned Eddie and Kate of the gargantuan meals they would be expected to eat, advising: 'Do try to eat up or else they will be disappointed!' In Tonga, remembered the Queen, they dig deep trenches and fill them with hot stones upon which sucking-pigs slow-cook for days with the hot sun blazing down upon the proceedings. On the day of the great feast one of these piglets, complete with curly tail and head, is placed before each guest as they sit beneath the shade of coconut and bamboo leaves. The Queen, a light eater at the best of times, was also given a turkey, two lobsters, a water melon, yams, bananas and a coconut for her personal consumption. 'They'll keep you quite cool,' the Queen told Eddie with a twinkle in her eye. He later discovered that beautiful, sparsely-clad Tongan maidens kept the temperature down by fanning guests with leaves throughout the meal which lasted for hours.

The Kents discovered that the Tongans were indeed big eaters and it was not surprising that their host, the King, weighed over thirty stone. Despite the unnerving sight of so much food – reputedly one thousand pigs were on the menu each day along with the same number of chickens, lobsters and dozens of turtles made into soup – they enjoyed the trip immensely. The only sadness was that they missed George's sports day and his performance, before the footlights, as a gnome in the school play.

They flew home via Toronto, an opportunity to see Kate's brother John and his family. There were now four children, two of which she had never met. Their new home was a farm outside the city named Stockingtop, after a landmark at Hovingham, and there was also an apartment in Toronto. Inside the old, colonial-style house there was another link with home: a water colour painting of Hovingham Hall and other touches which Kate recognized as her brother's nostalgic wish to have some reminders of his old home in the new.

The Kents were invited back to Canada the following July to open the Calgary Stampede. Eddie managed to get seven days leave from his army duties and they treated it as a private holiday.

It began with the newspaper headline they enjoyed most: 'The Kents hit town'. The Duke was made an honorary Chief of the Blackfoot tribe and given the name of 'Running Rabbit', an honour he may well have considered a dubious one to an honoured guest. He was assured, however, that it was a considerable compliment for, in the opinion of the tribe, a rabbit – the only animal an eagle cannot catch because of its speed – deserved great deference. There was no question about the merit of Kate's Blackfoot name. The tribe called her 'Pretty Woman'.

Later the Duke and Duchess both rode in the Stampede Parade behind the band of the Irish Guards and followed by the Royal Canadian Mounted Police. As one newspaper report put it: 'Running Rabbit and Pretty Woman rode into town in stetsons and cowboy gear while 200,000 palefaces roared approval.'

It was a splendid fun trip and they felt gloriously exhilarated and surprisingly uninhibited. The Duke even donned Indian clothes and joined in a war dance with Kate watching proudly along with the other 'squaws'. They were young, enjoying life and very much in love. It was as well they had such a happy week and could not foretell the future for their return to Britain began a cycle of events which brought them more than their share of tragedy and dark days.

At first all seemed well. Princess Marina greeted them full of news about the Wimbledon Tennis Championships which, as the enthusiastic President of the All England Lawn Tennis Association, she attended each year.

The Princess seemed the same as usual, her attractive, husky voice vibrant with interest as she gossiped about the tennis. Her son and daughter-in-law may have noticed, as her friends had, that she was frailer, more fine-drawn. But as Marina herself pointed out, she was sixty-one. 'We all grow old and we must face it,' she said on one occasion.

There had, for years, been a problem of intermittent falls. 'I'm always tumbling about,' she used to say, laughing at herself. 'Och, I'm so silly.' But now her left leg and arm were growing increasingly painful and, on 19 July 1968, for the first time since she had become part of the royal team, she cancelled a public engagement after a particularly bad fall. Finally she agreed with her doctors and worried family that she should enter hospital for tests. These revealed Marina had an inoperable brain tumour and her eldest son was told the illness was terminal. He had the distressing task of telling his wife and brother and sister who were deeply shocked by the suddenness of it all. They decided, at a family conference, that the Princess was not to be told she was dying. There would only be, at the most, six or seven months of life left for the beautiful Greek Princess who had become so much an integral part of British public life.

Not even her closest friends were told. But Noël Coward, always acutely perceptive, must have guessed. He went to see her at Kensington Palace: 'She was in bed and looked very papery,' he observed. 'I am worried about her. She was very cheerful, however, and we gossiped and giggled.'

Disappointed that she could not spend her summer holiday as usual with her sister Olga in Italy, Princess Marina agreed to the doctors' orders to rest quietly at Kensington Palace. Kate and Eddie agonized over whether to cancel their own holiday in Sardinia but decided, finally, that if they did it might arouse 'Min's' suspicions that her illness was not 'just rheumatism', as she supposed.

When they returned life went on as usual with Marina growing increasingly fragile, but as animated and sparky as ever when close friends and family called. On 23 August she felt well enough to drive out to Thatched House Lodge to spend a happy day with Alex and the children.

Two days later, on the anniversary of her husband's death, there was a family church service followed by a lunch party at Kensington Palace. Marina's old friend Zoia Poklewska, who had come up from the country, stayed on to spend the night. They spent the evening talking about old times; those two old friends who had known each other most of their lives. Then Marina said: 'I feel so tired . . . I think I will go to sleep now.' Sometime during the night she drifted into unconsciousness and, with her family at her bedside, she died the following morning, after a mercifully painless and tranquil end. 'Thank God my sweet Mama knew no pain or suffering. And now she is at peace,' wrote Princess Alexandra to her mother's friend Cecil Beaton.

He had known her since 1934 and recalled how the arrival in England of 'the strangely beautiful Princess Marina of Greece to marry our Prince George gave us all an excitement and stimulus it will be hard to forget . . . we soon knew she was a character of great gentleness and modesty with a natural gift for draught-manship and a love of music. She enjoyed the company of people with creative talent. Then one dark wartime night at a tragically early age she became a widow. For hours on end she remained speechless and motionless as she stared out of the window. The people grieved with her as they were to do all her life.

'It was difficult for her to become assimilated with British habits. She had not the knack of making friends easily or quickly but once she had given a friendship it was a serious and lifelong commitment .... Beautiful and romantic Princesses are a rare phenomenon today and their mere existence enhances. Even those who saw her a little were warmed by the knowledge that she was there; with Princess Marina's death that particularly lovely glow has gone from the land.' It was a marvellous tribute from a sensitive man and summed up precisely the impact Marina had always made.

Her children were devastated and it fell to Kate and Angus to strengthen and comfort them, as friends and relatives from all over the world arrived in London for the funeral service. But first there was something they had to do. The Duke of Kent, as head of the family, asked the Queen for permission to move his father's coffin from the royal vault in the Albert Memorial Chapel where it had lain for the twenty-six years since his funeral. By a strange coincidence it was on the anniversary of that day, the twenty-ninth of August, when people living within the precincts of Windsor Castle were asked to draw their curtains in the early evening. Then the coffin of Prince George, Duke of Kent, was slowly driven through the Great Park to the Royal Mausoleum at Frogmore where Victoria and Albert are buried. There, beneath a plane tree, two open graves stood waiting and into one of them the coffin was gently lowered.

Just as they had come for the happier occasions of her two elder children's weddings, so the royal relatives from Europe descended on Windsor. Queen Helen of Romania, of the same generation as Marina, sorrowfully arrived to attend her cousin's funeral. So, too, came the Dowager Queen Frederika of Greece, another cousin and her son and daughter-in-law, King Constantine and Queen Anne-Marie of the Hellenes. Prince Philip's sister Princess Margarita of Hohenlohe-Langenburg, another cousin, and ex-King Umberto of Italy were also among the mourners.

The Duke of Windsor flew in from Paris and was met by his nephew, the Duke of Kent, at London Airport. For the frail and ageing David it was a nostalgic journey to bid goodbye to his favourite brother's wife. She had entertained the Windsors to lunch at Kensington Palace after a ceremony commemorating Queen Mary's birth one hundred years before, only the previous summer, refusing to join her sister-in-law, the Queen Mother, in her vendetta against them.

During the funeral service in St George's Chapel, Princess Marina's children, Edward, Alexandra and Michael, sat with Kate and Angus Ogilvy in the choir stalls in front of the Queen, the Duke of Edinburgh, the Queen Mother and the Duke of Windsor. They had chosen Marina's favourite psalm 'The Lord is my Shepherd' and the hymn she had loved also, 'He Who Would Valiant Be'. Finally the choir sang 'God Be In My Head'. The Princess's coffin was draped with her personal standard and partly, also, by the blue and white flag of Greece. Her adopted country and the land of her birth were further represented by the presence of the Archimandrite Gregory Theodorus, Chancellor of the Diocese of Thyateira, who stood next to the Archbishop of Canterbury at the service.

Pall-bearers from the regiments of which Princess Marina had been Colonel-in-Chief – the Queen's Regiment, the Devonshire and Dorset Regiment and the Corps of Royal Electrical and Mechanical Engineers – carried the coffin from St George's Chapel. As they followed, close behind, Alexandra held a hand of each of her brothers. Behind them walked Kate with her brother-in-law, sadly conscious that the guiding wisdom of a true friend had gone from her life.

She had known her mother-in-law for just over ten years. As Cecil Beaton noted, Marina did not become intimate with anyone easily, however welcoming she appeared. After seven years as her mother-in-law, she had indeed become a second mother to Kate; one who, moreover, guided her expertly through the quicksands of royal protocol and the duties of her emerging public life as Duchess of Kent.

Perhaps if Princess Marina had been spared to live longer, some of the strain Kate was to suffer in the next decade might have been assuaged.

PART TWO

PART TWO

10

The Troubled Years

S he had been Duchess of Kent since the day of her marriage. But, compared to the immense popularity of her mother-in-law, Princess Marina – a foreigner totally accepted by the British – Katharine in the Sixties was hardly noticed by the public. A national poll found that she and her husband had 'apparently made little impact as yet ... the couple are not very well known', which was not surprising as they had been out of the country for several years.

Before Princess Marina's death, Kate had, in effect, been an understudy. Now, suddenly, she was plunged into an increasingly busy schedule of royal engagements – taking on many of the patronages formerly held by her mother-in-law and some, more-over, of the ailing Duke of Gloucester whose duties were being shared out around the family.

In February 1969, after the first of the three planning meetings for the year ahead, it was decided that the Duchess should become patron of the Spastics Society, an organization in which Princess Marina had been particularly interested. And in this, as with all the royal duties she would take on in the future, Kate made a considerable impact with her inherent warmth and charm.

By the time she realized, at the end of the year, that she was pregnant again with her third child, the Duchess had a diary packed with engagements and was blossoming happily as a junior member of the Queen's team.

She had been invited to fly out to Singapore and Hong Kong in early February 1970 – her first solo overseas trip – to visit WRAC and Army Catering Corps units and insisted that the tour went on – despite the fact that the Colonel-in-Chief was pregnant.

Home for her thirty-seventh birthday, she celebrated with her husband and the children, now seven and a half and nearly six, aware that a long separation from Eddie lay ahead. He was beginning a tour of duty with the United Nations peace-keeping force in Cyprus and this time Kate was staying at home to await her baby. For the first time, also, he was not with her for the birth which took place in hospital – safer, Sir John Peel, the royal gynaecologist, decided, for an older mother.

Katharine insisted on phoning her husband herself immediately after the birth to tell him he had a second son and third child, born thirteenth in succession to the throne on 25 July, in place of his cousin James Ogilvy – who moved down one to fourteenth. Prince Charles, then twenty-two, was a godfather to Nicholas Charles Edward Jonathan, the first Lord Windsor of the royal house of Windsor – the so-British name George V chose to take the place of the former Germanic titles during the First World War against Germany, whose armies were led by his cousin, the Kaiser.

Soon after Princess Marina's death the Queen had asked the Duchess of Gloucester (now Princess Alice) if she and her husband – who was incapacitated after a stroke – would like to move into her late sister-in-law's Kensington Palace apartments. This left York House, St James's Palace, free as a grace-and-favour town house for the Duke and Duchess of Kent who, because of their growing commitments on the royal rota, needed a London home. They would be occupying the rooms once used by the Duke of Windsor, as Prince of Wales, and his brother 'Georgie', later Duke of Kent.

For Katharine and Edward it meant a London base which eased their journeys to engagements considerably. York House became a much-loved home, especially as, like Coppins, it had associations with the Duke's father.

Another decision had, in fact, to be made about the Buckinghamshire home where Eddie, Alex and Michael had grown up. The village of Iver was gradually mushrooming around it, security was not easy and it was becoming increasingly expensive to maintain. They both felt the time had come to sell Coppins and get a country home further from London where they could really relax. Again the Queen helped, offering her cousins the lease of Anmer Hall on the Sandringham estate.

With three flourishing children Kate made no secret of her wish for more. 'I'd love a large family,' she told friends. All through the Seventies she worked hard as a member of the Royal Family and, in her private life, cherished the belief that she could combine her royal duties with further pregnancies.

But, in retrospect, did she try too hard to follow in Princess Marina's footsteps at the expense of her own private longing for another baby? 'Kate was very tense at that time,' observed one close to the Duchess, 'aware that she was growing older and time was passing by so quickly.'

In 1973, the year she had her fortieth birthday – a formidable landmark for any woman – her father, Sir William Worsley, died. For Katharine it was an appalling blow because there had been, between father and daughter, an exceptionally close and loving bond. Her mother, Joyce, was desolate, so unlike her old self and unable, at first, to come to terms with widowhood. So that bleak, personal year, not only had she lost a father who had, from the time she was a small girl, been a trusted confidante, but her mother who, since childhood, had been there to comfort and support was not her usual encouraging, stoical self.

But life, especially a busy royal one, goes on. After the summer holidays spent as usual with the children, Kate accompanied her husband – who had just been promoted to Lieutenant Colonel in the army – to Japan and Burma. It was a major tour which began with the opening of the British Export Marketing Centre in Tokyo. When they returned to England, Kate still felt the loss of her father acutely. Speaking of his death some years later she said: 'I loved him very deeply and I miss him very much as a person to talk to and confide in.'

Additionally, that third year of the Seventies, she fell victim to the first of the illnesses that would mar the rest of the decade – a gall bladder infection which caused her considerable discomfort and pain. Especially as, at first, she tried to struggle on and fulfil her engagements. After a period of treatment and rest, Kate went back to her royal round and completed a busy schedule of duties for the rest of the year. Those close to her knew she still hoped for more children and how concerned she was when an attack of German measles – potentially dangerous to an unborn child – laid her low for a time in the spring of 1975. Increasingly her health began to give cause for some anxiety and a year later, in March 1976, she entered King Edward VII Hospital for Officers, cancelling all engagements until the end of the month. At the time she was understood to be 'in need of a rest'. By the second week of April it had, by then, been announced that she was suffering from 'mild anaemia' and her engagements were cancelled for a further two weeks. That same month, the Duke – who had been upset by not being allowed to serve with his regiment in Northern Ireland – left the army.

It was a decision he had been pondering for several years because of increasing frustration with a job he nevertheless loved. His royal rank precluded him, on security grounds, from realizing his full potential as a soldier. This became all too apparent when fears for his safety resulted in the Duke being abruptly recalled from service in Ulster where his regiment was on a routine tour of duty.

Additionally there was a very real financial problem which had influenced the decision to part with their much-loved family home for an estimated £160,000 – a low figure by today's prices.

Like Prince Charles, his cousin turned to the Royal Family's grandfather figure, Earl Mountbatten, for counsel, explaining that what he really needed was a challenging job that would also help the family finances. Eddie was pessimistic, believing that the Queen would never agree to a royal prince taking a salaried position with a commercial firm. But already the sweeping changes which would eventually result in her own youngest son doing just that were under way. Fully briefed by 'Dickie' Mountbatten, the Queen encouraged her cousin's move into civilian life in a job which fulfilled the potential generated by the army and guaranteed a reasonable income with which to augment his Civil List allowance which was then quite modest.

Two months after leaving the army he became Vice-Chairman of the British Overseas Trade Board, a job which takes him all over the world promoting British trade. In that first year alone, he visited South America, Scandinavia, Germany and the United States.

The following June, 1977, Kate found to her joy that she was pregnant again. Expecting this fourth child at the age of forty-four – she would have been forty-five when the baby was due – it was normal to experience some valid fears because of the increased risk of pregnancy with an older mother. She was advised to rest and take life easier so she did not personally attend the British Congress of Obstetrics and Gynaecology which she had been due to address.

Instead her speech was read for her and her words to the gathering of experts showed that she had the morality of abortion on her mind at this time. She warned of the need to keep tight controls on abortion and pointed out that abuses of the abortion law could easily become standard practice. Human life was sacred and uniquely valuable; a gift from God that should never be taken for granted, she stressed.

Sadly her own pregnancy was not going smoothly. A few weeks later the Duchess felt unwell and her husband, who had been on an important diplomatic visit to Iran, rushed home to London. Looking weary and tense he drove her himself to the King Edward VII Hospital where doctors gave her an emergency examination. The next day the Queen's gynaecologist, Mr George Pinker, and the royal physician, Dr Richard Bayliss, said there were complications in the Duchess's pregnancy.

For thirty-six hours they battled to save the baby but it was in vain. Both Katharine and Eddie were deeply distressed and he left her bedside for a few moments only to call the one person he felt could give her some comfort – her friend, the Archbishop of Canterbury, Dr Donald Coggan. He spent about thirty minutes with husband and wife and they prayed together gaining some small measure of solace. For Kate it was an indescribably heart-breaking experience from which she did not fully recover psychologically for some years. 'It is God's will,' the sad Duchess said and turned increasingly to religion and the help of churchmen – among them the Rev John Andrew, then chaplain to the Archbishop. He became a close family friend and confidante and is still consulted as Pastor and adviser to the family, although living in America as Rector of Saint Thomas's Church, New York. His apartment on Fifth Avenue is sometimes used by the Kents when they are on a private visit to the city and signed photographs from them decorate the rooms.

As she endeavoured to recover from the miscarriage, the Duchess found that the roulette of life which had spun so disastrously for her recently was still ill-starred. In January, 1979, her mother, Lady Worsley, died in her sleep at Hovingham, aged seventy-four. 'Blue blood is just as red as anybody else's; the tears just as bitter' was a saying of Princess Marina's father, Prince Nicholas of Greece. It was one she sometimes quoted and Kate may have remembered it as she struggled on gamely after the funeral.

But the strain she was under was beginning to tell. During a visit to Manchester – to one of her favourite patronages the Royal Northern College of Music – the Duchess hesitantly mentioned to students that she had been unwell: 'I've been told by doctors not to exert myself. I have to go to bed early,' she said. She then cut short her visit, during a production of Wagner's *Das Rheingold*, because she felt so tired and ill. A close friend pointed out that she was also feeling desolate because her baby would have been born around that time. A relative suggested there was nothing seriously wrong. 'If there had been we would have heard.' He added: 'She has been pitching up well after losing the baby.'

But, unlike women living a purely private life, Kate could not go to ground for a while to recover in peace. Royals do not cancel engagements and this had been an unwritten rule since Queen Mary's day. Her inflexible attitude to duty still governed the family as did that of her daughter-in-law, the Queen Mother, whose invariable advice was: 'We must "grin and bear it".'

Katharine tried to pick up the threads of official life but the following month the gall bladder trouble flared up again. This time it was really serious; her doctors decided a major operation was necessary and back she went to King Edward VII Hospital. Afterwards she went straight to Windsor Castle, where the Queen had gone for her Easter break, to spend a few days recuperating. The Duke was away on an overseas trip and the Queen was genuinely concerned about his wife and felt she should not go home alone.

Despite being surrounded by concern and affection, Kate remained withdrawn and unhappy. Nothing, it seemed, could heal the suffering that was building up and beginning to produce symptoms that would have been so alien to the happy woman she had been before her miscarriage.

Whilst she struggled against the increasing deep depression and unresolved grief, friends and family grew daily more worried. One evening, in particular, highlighted how indisposed she was and brought matters to a head. The Kents gave a dinner party at York House and invited several old and close friends for a relaxed evening. It turned out to be 'anything but', as one of them put it. The Duchess came into the room exquisitely dressed, as usual, in a shimmering striped evening gown. 'But she was deathly pale with her hair looking quite grey, unlike its usual silvery blonde. All through dinner she sat, uttering not one word, miles and miles away. Then she rose silently from the table and left the room.'

It was so unlike the gracious woman they all knew, who would do anything to put people at ease and who took her duties as a hostess most conscientiously. It was, alas, only too clear that she was seriously disturbed and unwell. The anxious Duke called in doctors and, acting on their advice, the Duchess entered King Edward VII Hospital on 16 March suffering from 'nervous strain'. Wisely the Duke did not attempt to disguise the nature of the illness or conceal the fact that recovery might take some time. 'It will be weeks rather than days. There is still no time fixed for her coming out,' said his spokesman, Commander Richard Buckley, who had the unenviable task of coping with increasing media

115

curiosity and the bizarre and hurtful rumours that began circulating at this time.

Apart from medical treatment for her overwhelming depression, music was great therapy for Kate during this spell in hospital. Her husband showed devotion and sensitivity, visiting her every day and sometimes bringing their youngest child Nicholas who was not away at school like the others. They often listened to classical tapes together which helped them both, bridging the gulf which a depressive illness so often creates when the person affected retreats within themselves into a private world of pain and distress.

Coping gallantly with what must have been a traumatic and saddening experience for himself also, the Duke tried everything he could to help his wife, encouraging her on one occasion to slip out of hospital for a rehearsal of the Bach Choir in which – then and now – she sings soprano.

After seven long weeks in hospital, the Duchess left for home leaning on the Duke's protective arm for support. Even then, when she must have longed to escape the inevitable media interest, there was no way of avoiding it. She bravely faced up to reporters saying: 'I am still a little jaded – I'm afraid I can't stand for very long.'

On 16 May she was said to be making 'steady progress', quietly recuperating at home. But 'it is a long, slow haul back', said a member of her circle. 'The lights went out for a while.'

Rebuilding her life after the breakdown was helped by a long summer in Norfolk with her children who, although still quite young, were supportive and anxious to help. George, then seventeen, had been so concerned about his mother he had failed his exams at Eton but passed when he tried again, happier and more able to concentrate.

Helen, a bouncy fifteen year old had a talk with her mother's doctor and learnt how to understand her problems with the result that mother and daughter grew closer to each other that summer. When the holidays ended Nicholas, the youngest, went off to Westminster as a day boy instead of boarding at Eton, so that he could live at home. The fact that the 'nest' would not be entirely empty was an important factor in a recovery so dependent on the reassurance of a warm and loving family life.

In May, 1980, over a year later, a spokesman said: 'She is still playing herself back in' and, indeed, illness continued to haunt the Duchess well into the Eighties. The demons within her had been partially laid to rest but a displaced disc in her neck meant she had to wear a plastic collar at the Wimbledon tennis championships in 1981. Then, in April, 1982, she entered King Edward VII Hospital again, for the removal of a benign obstruction of the duct which links gall bladder to intestine. The following April, like a recurring spectre, illness struck again with a troublesome ovarian cyst which was removed at the same hospital. The Duchess took several months to recover from this operation with all her engagements at first only cancelled for five weeks and then extended for a further two months.

The swings and roundabouts of her oscillating depression combined with general ill health and the onset of the menopause made life very difficult for the whole family for nearly eight years and from time to time forced the Duchess back into hospital and out of public life. During one such spell a newspaper reported on 6 July 1983 that she was undergoing ECT – electro convulsive therapy, a method of tackling extreme depression. This report was denied and described as 'thoroughly unkind – a total fabrication', by the Kents' spokesman.

Be that as it may, the Duchess appeared greatly improved and herself effectively quelled further rumours by flying to the Greek island of Corfu with Eddie and the children for a sunshine holiday. During it Helen hit the headlines by sunbathing topless on a public beach. This 'shock-horror' revelation must have come as light relief to her parents when the British papers reached their island hideaway.

When the family returned home they went to spend the rest of the holiday at Anmer Hall. It is four miles from Sandringham and when they were younger the Kent children used to cycle or ride across the park, along the woodland road that locals call 'King's Avenue', to play with their cousins Andrew and Edward. The Hall, itself, is a typically English manor house whose imposing Georgian façade fronts a much older, beamed house where workmen once found a Priest's Hole – used in the days of religious persecution by the Duchess's ancestor Oliver Cromwell and his Puritans against the Roman Catholics. To Anmer Hall, then the home of the Walpole family, came a messenger from Kate's own home city of York with the news that a Jesuit son of the house had been martyred not far from the Minster.

From her Norfolk home the Duchess drove into King's Lynn to keep an appointment she had made to sing with the Bach Choir at the music festival. She appeared in fine voice and as one newspaper commented it was 'a brave effort to scotch rumours that were hurting her family'.

But the following week she slipped out of a concert by the Philharmonic Orchestra half-way through. 'She looked terribly tense. You can see it in her clenched hands. Everyone feels so sorry for her – she is such a lovely person,' said a fellow concert-goer.

Still she persevered, finding strength and comfort in Eddie, George, Helen and Nicholas who formed around her a protective circle. 'My mother only needs a rest – she is very tired,' Helen patiently told reporters who door-stepped her flat. Despite provocation the family were endlessly courteous and pleasant in what must have been a difficult time for them all.

Increasingly the Duchess turned to the solace of prayer and religion became even more important in her life. The shrine of Our Lady of Walsingham, near her Norfolk home, where for centuries men and women have prayed to be healed, was of especial comfort. She was a regular visitor, according to Father Alan Carefull of the Shrine Office. On these minor pilgrimages, the Duchess was sometimes accompanied by her eldest son George; sensitive and compassionate, he has always been close to his mother.

The Duchess's disturbed reaction to the miscarriage, followed by her mother's death, was not an unusual problem.

Doctor Katharine Dalton, specialist in woman's hormonal structure, said at the time that 'even a most determined woman, secure in a happy family cannot easily shrug off the dictates of her own body.' The same pattern of 'baby blues' that new mothers suffer can also strike after a miscarriage. Another doctor commented: 'If a woman has been trying for a baby for a long time or wants one before the menopause strikes, it is obviously harder to come to terms with a miscarriage.'

A malady, then, that affects many women but immeasurably more traumatic when it happens to a public figure who, when she is on duty, is the centre of all eyes. Private troubles do seem to be handled with less apparent stress by those born into the Royal Family, accustomed since early childhood to many people staring at them. Princess Anne may have felt unutterably sad during the break-up of her marriage, but her invincible will carried her through. On the other side of the coin, the born-royals are almost too controlled on occasions as shown by the Queen's and Princess Anne's outwardly unmoved, almost stony reaction to suffering children, although they are, without doubt, inwardly distressed. The Duchess of Kent and the Princess of Wales, both born commoners, show a gentle compassion with dying children that is infinitely touching.

Her own suffering made Kate sensitive to others and, as she would do in the future, she tried by small gestures to show how much she cared. One such occasion was at a service for eight lifeboatmen who lost their lives in 1981 in the Penlee disaster in Cornwall. Afterwards, in private, the Duchess distributed eight small crosses and chains she had chosen and had engraved with the date of the tragedy and a handwritten message – one for each bereaved family.

Gradually, as the healing months went by, her luminous smile and graceful elegance were seen more in public. Helen, for a time, 'stood in' as temporary lady-in-waiting so that she could be by her mother's side and help her through public engagements. As his brother and sister had shown, her children's support was all-important, and Nicholas, too, played his part. He accompanied his mother across the Atlantic to stay with her brother John and his family on their farm near Toronto. Kate loves Canada and for two weeks relaxed completely, enjoying the informal atmosphere of Stockingtop. She swam, played tennis, rode and just sunbathed, returning bronzed, glamorous and well on the way to recovery. The upward health spiral was completed by a visit to Forest Mere health farm where she walked around, totally relaxed, in jumpsuit and bare feet. The Duchess had turned the corner and grew steadily stronger. By the autumn she was back at work again with a light programme which gradually increased as she felt fitter and more confident. One of the tribulations of being royal is having to share any misfortune with the newspaper-reading public. But in her re-emergence into public life Katharine was greatly encouraged by the measure of affection and sympathy she received. Stories in national newspapers, television and news broadcasts welcomed her return to official engagements and those close to her knew how reassured she felt because of it.

But there was yet another piece of ill-health to contend with, in February, 1984. She had an operation for a hernia in King Edward VII Hospital. Soon after Princess Margaret offered Kate and Eddie the loan of her house on Mustique in the West Indies for a sunshine holiday. They returned looking bronzed, fit and happy.

Others who have emerged from what Virginia Woolf called 'the dark cupboard of illness' – particularly a serious depressive one – have noticed that when the inner pressure lifted, they seemed more aware; more perceptive of weakness and despair in others. For Kate it gave her an added insight into the job she now does so wholeheartedly, as patron of charities such as the Samaritans, the Hospice Movement and the Cancer Appeal Macmillan Fund amongst others.

Psychotherapy has been described as a cleansing of the system and by undergoing such treatment, as it was reported she did, the Duchess would have found greater understanding not only of herself but others. The actor Jeremy Brett telling Marilyn Willison of his recovery from a nervous breakdown said: 'I've had the scales dropped from my eyes as a result of the episode. I can tell the state of others' well-being now. When you've been there you get an added insight ...'

Certainly Katharine Kent, at a turning point in her life,

appeared to develop a deep commitment to put something back. To atone, perhaps, for her troubled years – when she deeply worried those she loved – and began to benefit others by her own experience. She had emerged a fighter, a survivor and no longer a victim.

11

Turning Point

It was evident that a heightened spiritual awareness aided the
Duchess of Kent's return to the public arena. She gained
enormous strength from her years of extreme vulnerability and
accepted a changed attitude to both personal and public life. At
the same time she made effective use of the experience gained
during her period of distress and ill-health. As she herself put it:
'I don't believe there is anyone in the world who hasn't suffered
something. All of us have one cross to bear and it is through
these experiences that one learns empathy and compassion.'

In the maturity of her late fifties, the Duchess appears to have
developed an almost mystical devotion to the elderly, the sick
and the helpless; has found in suffering and dying the qualities
which move her most. These men, women and children are
victims and having been one herself, for a time, she wants, more
than anything, to befriend them not in a sentimental sense but to
offer practical help such as the care given by the organizations of
which she is very much a working patron.

One cause that is especially close to her heart is the Samaritans,
the movement founded by the Rev Chad Varah to help the suicidal
and despairing. When she was asked to become patron, the
Duchess determined to see if she herself could become a Samaritan. She believes in being thoroughly involved when she takes
on a patronage, rather than merely being a name on a letterhead.
So she took the twelve weeks' training course at a central London

branch along with a group of ten volunteers from all walks of life.

All of them, including Katharine, had the simple, basic quality needed in a Samaritan: that of being a human being. As Simon Armson, Assistant General Secretary explained, this can be extended by 'sharing your humanity with someone else in distress and being prepared to absorb that distress and help someone through it'.

The Duchess put it another way: 'You listen – you honestly just listen. Often this is the first time anyone has.' She found she had a personal reservoir which could assimilate other people's unhappiness and grew used to talking about death and suicide. Her interest developed 'passionately' and at the end of her training the Duchess did a regular weekly four-hour shift, sitting and just waiting for the telephone to ring.

She was acutely conscious now of the world of misery, suffering and despair which lay outside the enclosed royal world of privilege, wealth and comfort. 'Some people are naturals; some need to learn warmth. The Duchess is a natural,' said the General Secretary, Joan Burt.

Sometimes the caller panics and puts the receiver down. Or Katharine found she was holding on to the phone for over an hour waiting for the distressed person to speak, just saying occasionally ... 'I'm here if you want me.' It was easier to help if she put herself in their position. 'In a way we hold their hand. You also try hard to find in their life some glimmer of light they can catch on to,' said the Duchess. It could be news of a friend, the prospect of a visit from a relative or an outing with a local club – just something to look forward to with interest.

Some of the cases the Duchess dealt with gave her insight and experience which no other member of the Royal Family has. She now knows what life is like at rock bottom because she has learnt it at first hand. 'She loosens people up by being so normal,' observed Linda Marsh of the Samaritans. 'She has a personal serenity – not plastered on.'

Because the callers are nearly always at their lowest ebb they are often inarticulate or sobbing into the telephone. There is always the fear they may be one of the 5,000 suicides recorded each year – a worrying cause of death in Britain. One person kills himself every two hours; someone tries to take their own life every two and a half minutes and statistics in the under-twenty-five group are steadily increasing.

Sometimes, as the Duchess learnt, the call could be from someone just starting on the downhill path of depression that can lead eventually to suicide, particularly at times like Christmas and New Year. Nothing, it seems, accentuates misery more than too much of other people's happiness. Strangely, spring and early summer, which usually make people feel happier, have the highest suicide rate – in April, May and June.

Despair is not just an urban problem as the Duchess, herself, has pointed out: 'How would we ourselves like to spend the long winter nights alone in a remote country village waiting for the daylight to return?' she asked. So the Samaritans go to county shows where a surprising number of people visit their tent. They found there is a lot of unhappiness in the countryside, particularly in the more remote parts. Samaritans are also now helping prison inmates and educational bodies. Katharine is also Patron of Befrienders International which has extended the work to the four corners of the world.

Like all the Samaritan volunteers, Kate learnt totally to focus her attention and concentration on a call which might be from an ill-treated child, an elderly person who had not seen another soul for days, a teenager with a drug problem or someone who has just been told they were terminally ill. They all have the same desperate need to talk to someone.

This is often more difficult than it seems and it was the average person's inability to speak about the things that really matter to them, to bring them to the surface and share with others, that inspired Chad Varah in the first place. From one small branch in his City of London church, St Stephen's Walbrook, his organization has grown to 2,000 branches with 22,000 volunteers. Among them, for a time, was Katharine Kent who had, by then, graduated into being a good listener, as perceptive and understanding as any of them. 'She has a warm-hearted compassion that is totally natural,' said Simon Armson and in his concept of a Samaritan, the prototype he described could have been the Duchess herself, after her emergence from personal misfortune.

It is no bad thing, according to Simon, for volunteers to have their own history of emotional problems. They should be 'not someone who hasn't suffered in the past, who doesn't bear some scars of that sort but someone who's got stability now, not only to be at peace with themselves, but also to share the distress of others'.

Because of her close links with the Samaritans it would be tempting to speculate that Kate herself received help from the organization when she most needed it during her depressive illness. But as the solid bedrock of their work is total confidentiality, that is one royal secret that will never be revealed.

Among the problems confronted by Samaritans are mental illness, bereavement, Aids, incest, sexual problems or addiction. Occasionally a counsellor puts down the telephone after a particularly traumatic call feeling totally drained and so distressed, personally, that he or she has to be comforted and reassured by a colleague.

The Duchess believes fervently in the work of the Samaritans and travels all over the country visiting the 200 branches. 'Often if she's got another engagement in the district and finds she has a few minutes to spare, she'll pop into a branch unexpectedly,' said Linda Marsh. 'Then she is quite likely to pick up the telephone herself if it rings while she is around. She has the ability within seconds of meeting or speaking to someone, to make them feel an old and trusted friend.'

Twenty-two thousand volunteers, like Kate, cope with over two million calls a year. They are 'people who can listen compassionately and who are willing to give support to anyone who is lonely, frightened, in trouble or has come to the point when they feel life is no longer worth living'. One of the Duchess's aims in her work for the Samaritans is to help increase the number of volunteers which are wanted desperately.

As she is so committed to an increasing workload, Kate no

longer does her weekly stint with the Samaritans although she hopes to find time in the future. But, as she told members of the organization, 'having once worked as a volunteer I find myself always alert to any problems which I see or hear of during many aspects of my working day'.

Whatever the trouble, Samaritans are not there to solve problems or offer advice. Katharine, along with all the other volunteers, was taught to befriend and, by listening, to help. Often a caller is asked to visit the office and then the ability to listen must be coupled with the use of body language. This aspect of the training has helped the Duchess with some of her other charities like Age Concern where, simply by holding someone's hand, as she always does, she conveys so much warmth and sympathy.

She does reach out to touch people a lot; perhaps by holding an old lady's hand, stroking the arm of another or cuddling an ailing child. Kate finds it comes naturally to comfort a pensioner grieving for her dead husband by holding her close and murmuring 'Don't cry ... don't cry', as she did in Martyn Lewis's mini-documentary for the BBC about Age Concern. Or going to the sink and washing up a dirty cup so that she could give an elderly woman a much-needed cup of tea. 'It was not contrived at all,' Martyn told me. 'The Duchess saw a dirty cup and quite naturally washed it up, along with some other things. She is totally natural on television, making the camera a genuine observer – not a catalyst as some people do.'

The Duchess will always remember an elderly couple who lived in a high rise block at the time of frequent power cuts. 'I suddenly wondered how they were coping.' The old lady was bedridden but her husband managed to do the shopping for them both. But only, of course, if the lifts were working. The Duchess, watching the flickering candlelight in York House and the surrounding buildings, realized this. 'I went round to see them and found that no one had been near them for two whole days. So for forty-eight hours they'd had no food at all.' She was horrified by the situation and personally saw to it that the old couple had provisions and heat in their lonely eyrie high above the London street.

It is this instinctive wish to help in a practical way that is so admirable and wins Kate so many devoted allies, not least her own ladies-in-waiting. They have seen it many times before but still marvel at the gentle way she deals with unhappy situations. 'You couldn't give so much in the way she does without feeling deeply,' said lady-in-waiting and former personal secretary, Sarah Partridge, whose job included helping the Duchess keep in touch with all the lonely, distressed and terminally ill people whose trust and affection she has won and with whom, according to Sarah, 'she is so magical'.

Because of her past illnesses she is far from robust and so it is the quality not the quantity of engagements that is top priority. Her staff know that she gives so much that she sometimes gets home completely exhausted, emotionally drained but so happy. The traumas of the lives – of the young and old she meets in her work – seem to leave her with nothing but fulfilment. If she feels the slightest strain, sometimes, she 'raids the larder' to relax a bit or talks the day over with her husband.

As the Duchess is the link between several caring organizations, she tries to inter-relate them so that their impact can be even stronger, occasionally by a shared party. 'She is very tactile,' said Simon Armson, 'keen for her own charities to get together and collaborate.'

One such instance is the way in which the Samaritans can help Age Concern care for the elderly. 'In an ideal world old age should be serene and peaceful and each individual should feel not only an inner contentment at the completion of life's work but should be surrounded also by a family who will cherish them and turn to them for guidance from their wider experience of years passed and knowledge gained. Alas, how rare is this dream realized in practice,' points out the Duchess.

'Their loneliness must at times be intense. Who should these people turn to if the need arises – the Samaritans? I myself would indeed be happy to be the first to initiate this idea in my own locality.' By this the Duchess meant Westminster, near her London home, York House in St James's Palace. She pops 'round the corner' to see senior citizens where they get together for companionship and relaxation arranged by Age Concern. Kate plays darts – 'Make sure everybody gets out of the way,' she warns, and then throws a 'nifty arrow', as one pensioner put it. Sometimes she takes her turn handing out cups of tea or gently guiding a frail old lady to the dining table to have 'a good hot meal'.

'She leaves a wonderful glow behind and they discuss her visit for weeks afterwards. They love talking to her and I do believe the Duchess enjoys it too,' said one of the helpers.

Remembering, perhaps, her own parents, the Duchess – in one of her rare speeches – told a conference of the Samaritans in her home city of York, only twenty miles from Hovingham where she grew up: 'I love old people and they need loving. Every human being from birth to old age needs someone to befriend them; understand them; console them. A friend with whom to share life's problems and joys. It is not only the Samaritans who should be available.

'It is anyone who is prepared to listen to a neighbour in distress. People want to look after the elderly – I know that because after a brief programme on television when I highlighted the problems of three elderly people in one area of London, they were inundated with offers of free holidays, weekly visits and much else besides. So the will is there. How do we harness it? That is a matter for Age Concern. Our challenge as Samaritans is somehow to reach those thousands of people who desperately need our help but don't yet know where to look for it. We must all learn to listen for the quiet signals of despair.'

Unlike some do-gooding reformers, the Duchess underlines her dedication with an extraordinary personal charm which works its magic in all walks of life. 'She radiates a love and warmth that is tangible,' Caroline Oliver of Age Concern told me. 'With a sense of belief in what she does – in being a good person.'

Like the Samaritans, Age Concern is manned by volunteers who all care deeply about the plight of the elderly. 'This is an Age Concern,' said Kate pointing to herself as she listened to the needs of an old lady who just wanted someone to chat to – even if it was only once a fortnight. The Duchess regularly visits pensioners, sometimes in their homes or at the community centres set up for them, particularly her own 'local' one.

Katharine suffers herself from poor circulation and can sympathize with feeling cold – one of the most common problems experienced by the elderly. Simple needs of life can be a trial also and when pensioners show her their inadequate washing and toilet arrangements, the Duchess does not hesitate to inspect everything carefully for herself. Knowing some of the problems, therefore, she takes a great interest in the schemes which enable old people, who may be disabled and unable to get a wheelchair into their own bathroom, to visit day centres. There, once a week, they can enjoy the luxury of a bath. 'Getting into warm water is something many of our "customers" have not experienced for months or even years,' said a helper at the Hove, Sussex, Age Concern centre.

In the last few years Katharine has had a unique opportunity, as she moves around in every strata of society, to form her own picture of the difficulties that quilt the counterpane of modern complacency in a world obsessed with material benefits. One of her beliefs is that, as industry and commerce become more technologically minded and organizations grow immense and impersonal, men and women lose the individual, caring touch they once had with their fellow human beings. 'However large and sophisticated our organizations may become, great resources and size do not by themselves provide all those services without which a society cannot call itself civilized,' she pointed out. It is very easy to forget in a busy life the people who have no work to fill up their day because they are too old. 'So many of the elderly, however uncomplaining, experience loneliness, illness, financial problems, boredom, lack of consuming interest or hobby, depression and often feel themselves to be a burden to friends and relatives. All this and much more can lead them to the point of suicide,' said the Duchess. Then she added the chilling reminder: 'Successful suicides are much more common among the elderly. Elderly people may say "without my wife, I have no reason to live" or "I am too much of a burden to my children". Often the response is "Come on now, you have plenty of good years ahead". This sort of answer seldom reassures; instead the elderly person feels guilty, ungrateful and thinks here is just one more person who does not understand. This is not what they deserve in the last years of their life.'

But amidst the problems old age brings, the Duchess also finds great humour and cheerfulness. And, along the way, those gems of nostalgia remembered by the very old. Like Mr Jim Goodison, aged one hundred and five, who painted a picture for her of London long ago.

Katharine met him at a 'Not Forgotten' Association Christmas party in the Royal Mews, a yearly engagement she always attends as their patron. She obviously enjoyed meeting Mr Goodison, a former corporal who joined the army in 1902, three months after the Boer War ended. He wore a perky bow tie, paper hat and a flower in his buttonhole and regaled her with anecdotes of the Edwardian era he remembered so well. The old soldier initially greeted his royal visitor with a formal handshake; but she, in the way she does, put both hands over his as they talked, immediately making warm and responsive contact as she encouraged him to live, for a while, in the past. A picture of the London of his youth emerged as he recalled Queen Victoria's Diamond Jubilee in 1897 and – his earliest memory – of Hackney paperboys calling out that Jack the Ripper 'had done another one'.

That yearly meeting with old soldiers is always a cheery Christmas party and one she enjoys telling her soldier husband about when she returns to York House. She greets them, usually, with a 'thumbs up', using both hands and, in an immensely popular gesture, distributes cans of beer all round! 'That lady is pure gold,' said one of the old campaigners. 'I'll lift my glass to her health, any day.'

There are so many facets to the Duchess's working life as the many hundreds of notes filed away in the office at York House testify. But in over eighty personal patronages and commitments, initiating her own crusade to help those in trouble and highlighting the problems of old age rank high in her list of priorities. Increasingly she shows how the breadth of her vision and experience has expanded since her own troubled years. Her vocation now encompasses the helpless at each end of life's journey – the oldest and youngest among her cousin-in-law, the Queen's, subjects.

12

Tears and Smiles

The sparkling woman with the swept-back silver blonde hair wore a simple green tunic over a striped cotton dress. But in her ears were small jewels that reflected the light brilliantly. The same stones, set in gold, were on her wrist. The eyes of fragile children followed the Duchess of Kent as she moved amongst them, her smile lighting up the room full of youngsters which should have been noisy and full of high spirits, as a normal gathering of children would have been.

Instead it was quiet and controlled because these children were desperately ill with no hope of a future. But the jewellery the royal visitor was wearing fascinated them as she knew it would and it was why she wore it on one of her many informal visits to Helen House, Oxford – Britain's first children's hospice. One young girl especially loved the earrings. In the carefree days when she was well, she had her ears pierced. Now, suffering from a brain tumour, earrings were still her pride and joy, as the Duchess knew when she took off her own, on her last visit, and gave them to the child.

Next time Kate visited Helen House she was greeted with the words: 'I've got your Duchess earrings on.' 'I can see you have,' said the Duchess, who had not forgotten how thrilled she had been with the present and brought her another pair of her own which she fixed in the young patient's ears. 'Do you remember last time we talked at lunch, you said to me, "Do you wear a

132

crown?" and I said, "Only Queens wear crowns",' said the Duchess.

Her work at Helen House has taught her that, sadly, the loving joy that welcomes a new baby into the world is inevitably absent when the child leaves it, prematurely, because of a tragic terminal illness. The strain of nursing can sap a family's energy and comprehension, however devoted they may be. But it need not be like that as parents who find shelter for their stricken children in Helen House do find. There, in Katharine's own words: 'Tears and smiles so often walk side by side.'

Her own radiant smile seems to inspire and encourage the children who gaze at her adoringly on her many morale-raising visits to the Hospice, created by Mother Frances Dominica with donations raised in the summer of 1980. Kate goes to Helen House whenever she can find a few hours, to join the eighteen dedicated helpers who care for eight children at a time. Like everyone who enters it she is immediately aware of the remarkable atmosphere that has been created in this sanctuary for tragic children and their parents. 'It's one of the happiest places I know,' she says.

The truism that laughter and sorrow lie close together is evident at Helen House. So is the communion that seems to exist between members of the caring professions; those selfless people who cope with imminent or prolonged dying and who know, as Katharine Kent invariably shows with every gesture, that a soothing, loving touch or gentle words can break down the barriers, particularly with a very sick child.

The Duchess puts on one of the sleeveless green tunics that all the helpers wear, when she visits the Hospice. Her volunteer colleagues are nurses, social workers, physiotherapists, a chaplain and several parents. All are chosen because they love children and understand that, more than anything, terminally ill youngsters need cherishing. And, when the time comes to die, warmth and love, surrounded by family and caring friends they may have met since their illness.

Sometimes, the Duchess has been there also, close to the end, comforting both the child and the parents. One such case was a very special small boy who had visited Helen House and in whose case Katharine had become personally involved, as she so often does. She had told him she was going to Australia – on an official visit – and promised to bring him back a toy koala bear. But on the morning the Duke and Duchess were due to leave, she had this overwhelming feeling that she should visit him at Great Ormond Street Children's Hospital where he had been transferred. The Duke argued, saying she would never be back for the flight, so she went at 6.30 am to see the child, taking her own koala bear to give to him. Although it was early the hospital was awake; the night shift preparing to hand over and young patients rousing to face a new day. But a small group gathered round the bed as the Duchess arrived, already feared there would be only a few hours left for the boy who lay there.

The Duchess spoke softly to him and he knew she was there. He had told her on an earlier occasion: 'I know that I'm going to die. I'm not afraid.' Adding: 'I only hope I'm not around when it happens.' He was pleased with his koala bear and after a few minutes at his bedside Katharine hugged the parents and Mother Frances, who had travelled from Oxford to be there – another reassuring, familiar face.

She had been only just in time and her premonition was, sadly, justified. As they boarded the aircraft she received a message from Mother Frances that her young friend had died.

To raise much needed funds for Helen House, formed entirely by voluntary contributions, the Duchess agreed to make a film for ITN and became the first member of the Royal Family to walk around with a radio mike attached to her tunic so that every word she said was recorded over a three- to four-hour period. 'It showed a very high degree of trust,' said presenter Martyn Lewis who is now a devoted admirer of the Duchess's work. He, himself, has done much to help take away the fear of the unknown by writing a book about hospices and, with sensitive television programmes, explaining how they work.

As she spoke to the sick children, Katharine's voice was not hushed but strong and vibrant; she radiated vitality and serene happiness so that the youngsters blossomed under her spell.

'The Duchess is inspirational in hospices,' observed her lady-in-waiting, Mrs Claire Wilmott-Sittwell. 'I still find myself amazed at the effect she has.'

Katharine's small, bright presence moves around Helen House. Sometimes she sings with the children, her fine clear soprano rising above their childish voices. She greets parents arriving with a desperately ill child explaining that Helen House is there to lighten their burden and let them have some rest. 'We are here to help you so don't feel you are asking too much. Nothing is too much here at Helen House,' she said.

Often parents tend to avoid the hospices, as though by seeking help they are admitting their own failure. But Mother Frances has shown that she and her staff can help throughout a child's illness – not just in caring for the patient but in trying to heal the agony of parents.

It is not only during their child's short lifetime they need comfort – but afterwards when bereavement counsellors help to bridge the traumatic gap.

The object of Helen House is not to take children permanently. It is there to fill a much-needed gap: to take care of children when their parents need a rest. Or there are special flats where the whole family – even much-loved pets – can be together and mothers and fathers can help as much as they wish. Sometimes, however devoted they are, the rest of the family may need a complete break and, in this case, the staff at Helen House will look after their sick child with love and care until he or she goes home again. There is no charge but children do need their doctor's approval to travel.

The Oxford hospice is no longer alone in the field. There are now three other hospices for children in Britain, modelled on the example of Helen House and others are in the planning stage, helping to make Britain a leader in hospice care for the under-sixteens.

Trying to lift the load from the miserable and ill, the old and the helpless has been a vocation for royal princesses since the Middle Ages. But getting so specifically involved, as the Duchess of Kent does, is not so usual.

Princess Anne, who sees much widespread suffering in her tireless work for the Save the Children Fund, admits she cannot get too close to individual cases. 'I would just go nuts. You have to stay remote otherwise you would crack up,' she has pointed out in a personal interview.

Day by day, as she moves around the country, it is becoming clear that Katharine's mission lies in doing just that. Her participation in the world, outside the protected, rarified milieux of the court, where she has found so much human tragedy and suffering, is dedicated and increasingly knowledgeable. The example of her cousin-by-marriage has helped the Princess of Wales overcome the distress she feels when she visits hospitals and hospices. Diana is often moved to tears and cries bitterly in the car going home. But in coming to terms with the plight of children she meets she has found it helpful to learn from Katharine's experiences and the older woman has 'talked her through' to a greater understanding of terminally ill patients. There is an attitude of mind, as Katharine has learnt, in approaching such cases – calmly, compassionately and, above all, without apprehension.

Diana was particularly upset by the death of fifteen-year-old Claire Bosworth from Derbyshire whose last wish was to meet the Princess of Wales.

Claire was taken from her bed to make a 130-mile journey by wheelchair to the Champion Children's awards in London. Diana knelt by her chair, obviously very moved, as Claire whispered: 'I'm just so cross I can't get out of this chair to curtsey to you.' The Princess heard how she had succeeded in passing seven CSE examinations whilst undergoing painful chemotherapy and radiation treatment. She was 'deeply upset' said a member of her staff, when she heard of Claire's death shortly afterwards. The Princess wrote to Mrs Bosworth – a handwritten note which was heartfelt and 'just like a letter from one mum to another'.

As the Princess of Wales becomes more and more interested in a vocation for good, she could not fail to be inspired by the Duchess's more in-depth approach to what many now regard as her calling in life. Martyn Lewis, who had the opportunity during the nine days of filming at Helen House to watch her closely, observed: 'What knocks down everyone is how down to earth and ordinary she is.' But, he added significantly, 'the reaction of suffering people is incredible. They seemed to lose ten years as she spoke to them. It is an almost spiritual effect.'

The Duchess's charities abound with stories about their patron. Going round a hospice in the Midlands she carried a wicker basket filled with small china angels which she had bought specially to give to each patient. At another she was presented with a bouquet of flowers and, instead of taking them home, she gave a flower to each person as she moved around. Susan Butler of Cancer Relief Macmillan Fund, of which the Duchess is patron, said she conveys 'tremendous warmth and generosity of spirit' wherever she goes. 'She finds patients funny and brave and therapeutic,' she said. Then, perceptively, 'They have helped her as much, perhaps, as she has helped them.'

It is this ability to give something back that is becoming so characteristic of the Duchess. 'She immediately wins confidence and trust – she is never repetitious or trivial,' added Susan Butler. She remembers a visit to Mount Vernon Hospital, Middlesex, when the Duchess arrived with a birthday cake, still in its Harrods box, which she had stopped off to buy on the way, remembering that for one cancer patient, Edith Agar, it was a special day. The cake was Kate's own personal gesture to help her celebrate her birthday in hospital. The Duchess carefully placed and lit candles and then helped blow them out.

At the Royal Berkshire hospital she arrived to open a giant thermometer, recording money given to the Fund, with her hand heavily bandaged. 'I cut it with the bread knife,' said the Duchess matter-of-factly, hopping athletically over a small brick wall when the mechanism for the curtains failed to open them herself.

On another occasion, on a visit to Lingfield School, Surrey – where students with special needs including epilepsy, learning difficulties and other neurological disorders are helped to reach their full potential – all the children were waiting for the arrival of the royal helicopter. There was a flurry of cherry blossom as the Duchess stepped from it, covering her in confetti-like petals like a bride.

But then, as she started a walkabout, she was showered with torrential rain. Ignoring it she serenely continued to meet the excited children, unworried at the damage to her smooth, elegant hairstyle and lightweight check suit. She stopped by young Paul Collington, gallant as a courtier as he asked: 'May I kiss your hand?' 'Yes, certainly,' said the Duchess, her eyes twinkling. After he had done so she repaid the compliment by taking his hand and giving it a quick mock kiss to much laughter from the children.

Another child, overcome with the excitement of the day, impetuously flung her arms round the smiling Duchess and was warmly hugged back. Then she breezed in, out of the rain, to a room where students learn office and computer skills. They were all tense, waiting to meet her and she must have known for she shook the raindrops out of her hair and laughed cheerfully, dispelling their nervousness. 'Just look at me! I've been washing my hair out there – I'm absolutely drenched.' Behind her Sarah Partridge, the lady-in-waiting on duty, laughed too – and, very gently, pushed two big, decorative hair ornaments on the Duchess's head that had been falling out back into place.

On another rainy day at St Margaret's Hospice, Taunton, a large crowd was waiting for the Duchess, despite the elements. To everyone's surprise she left her car and, instead of going inside to meet the 'chain gang' – the mayor and other notables – she turned round and, in terrible weather, did a mini walkabout. 'You've been waiting all this time in the rain. It's the very least I can do,' she told the crowd. 'She comes across as a very genuine person,' said Diane Trembath of Help the Aged. 'She radiates a love and warmth that is tangible.'

Martyn Lewis believes the Duchess cannot do too much to try and communicate her caring. 'In many ways she is driving herself on to enormous breadth of commitment,' he said. At times, it seems, there is a fragile, vulnerable look about her that hints of past troubles; an air of remoteness when she is not actually 'on stage'. It contrasts with the warmth that comes so spontaneously with the young, the old and the sick.

13

Family Lady

Those close to Katharine knew she was longing to be a grandmother and her eldest son 'Georgie' and his wife Sylvana did not keep her waiting too long. Soon after they arrived in Budapest where he was taking up a short-term diplomatic post, following their marriage in January, 1988, George telephoned his parents in great excitement to give them the news. The infant Baron Downpatrick was born with his mother's large dark eyes, an unmistakable Windsor mouth and the squarish face shape of the Worsley men on 2 December 1988, eleven months after his parents' registry office wedding.

Kate hurried round to see him on the crisp winter morning following his birth in London and when she held her first grand-child in her arms she may well have felt some of the pain and years of grief for her own lost child eased.

The newest member of the family was born a commoner although he has the courtesy title of Baron Downpatrick and will, one day, inherit the royal Dukedom of Kent. But because of his great-great-grandfather King George V's edict that the title of Prince and Princess would only be granted to the child or grandchild of the Sovereign, he will never be styled His Royal Highness like his grandfather, the present Duke of Kent.

He is, however, in direct line to the throne. He was eighteenth at birth but he has since moved down to nineteenth with the birth of Princess Eugenie, daughter of the Duke and Duchess of York and the Queen's sixth grandchild.

George and Sylvana's son is far enough removed from the throne, like his father and Gloucester, Phillips and Harewood cousins, and need not endure the same disciplined lifestyle as those within the Queen's immediate family circle.

'Fortunately I am never going to carry out engagements like my parents. I have managed to remain anonymous so far in life and I want to stay that way,' said George St Andrews (nicknamed Stan by his schoolfriends because of his initials) when he was still in his teens. He emerged briefly from his anonymity to marry, amid much inevitable publicity, a Roman Catholic divorcee, Sylvana Tomaselli, whom he had met at university. Their first child, a direct descendant of William the Conqueror and a long line of European Kings and Queens including Queen Catherine the Great of Russia, became the first royal child to be cared for by both his parents who take turns to look after him when the other is working.

Commoner or not the baby had a royal christening in the Chapel of St James's Palace, conducted by family friend, the Right Reverend Michael Mann, Dean of Windsor.

He was named Edward (after his Kent grandfather and great-great-great-grandfather King Edward VII) Edmund Maximilian (after his Tomaselli grandfather) George (after his father, great-great-grandfather King George V and great-great-uncle King George VI). George and Sylvana appropriately linked the Royal Family and the Worsley family in their choice of godparents with the Princess of Wales as godmother and William Worsley, eldest son of Sir Marcus – the Duchess's brother – as godfather.

Her grandson's baptism and subsequent christening party at York House came just the day after Kate had been given the freedom of the city of York at a ceremony in the Minster. There, twenty-eight years before, she had married the Duke of Kent and become a member of the Royal Family.

'Such a happy weekend,' the Duchess beamed, as she presided over the party in the salon of York House with its apricot walls, willow green sofas and family photographs clustered on the old antique pieces, some of them collected by George and Marina, the baby's great-grandparents, so many years before.

Her youngest son Nicholas and her brother Marcus, the Lord Lieutenant of North Yorkshire, had escorted her to York Minster the day before. They heard the Lord Mayor of her home city say she had shared her joy and sorrow with them and enriched the lives of many.

The Archbishop of York pointed out the family feeling which existed between the Duchess and the people of York. 'We are here to honour a friend, a Duchess whom we proudly regard as part of our Yorkshire family. Surely it is precisely because she belongs already that she enjoys a freedom among us – a freedom which today's ceremony simply ratifies and confirms ... She belongs because she is always ready to come back and bring a touch of graciousness into the lives of the people.' But to the Duchess it was more than that. 'Yorkshire is a thread running through her life,' said Sarah Partridge, her lady-in-waiting, who is still amused by the words of the man from the *Yorkshire Post*. He delivers the newspaper daily to York House so that Katharine can keep up with local events. 'A good Yorkshire paper from a good Yorkshire man to a good Yorkshire lass,' he said – a remark which delighted the Duchess.

On the day she was given the Freedom Kate was clearly touched at being so honoured by the men, women and children of York whom she evidently regards as being part of her extended family. She chose to share her happiness, as usual, with the very young and the old. Spotting four-year-old Gemma Hale of Rose Street in the crowds, the Duchess made her day by stopping for a chat. She told her how much she envied her tucked up in a full-length coat. 'I bet you are nice and warm in that big coat,' she said. 'I'm not – I was very cold in that big church.' Then Katharine went to name a sheltered housing complex for the elderly and disabled in the city.

Her own children have been brought up with their Yorkshire heritage very much to the fore. They know their mother's childhood home well and have spent many happy holidays at Hovingham or Anmer Hall in Norfolk with their Worsley cousins of the same generation – the children of Kate's three brothers. The close friendship between William, heir to the Hovingham estate, and George resulted in his being asked to be a godfather to the Kent baby.

As far as their royal background is concerned the Duke and Duchess have always impressed upon George, Helen and Nicholas that, although they have the same royal ancestry, they would always have to earn a living. Staying frequently amid the grandeur of the Queen's homes – Windsor or Sandringham at Christmas; Balmoral in the summer – they were always told to remember their normal lifestyles must be based on less exalted planes.

But it could not have been easy trying to bring up children under those circumstances. Sir Angus Ogilvy, Princess Alexandra's husband, summed it up to journalist Audrey Whiting: 'It's very difficult for the children when they go back to school at the end of the holidays. They are inevitably asked where they went and they can only reply truthfully, "Balmoral" or "Windsor Castle". You can imagine what happens then. They are bombarded with questions such as "What is the Queen really like?"; "Do you eat with the Queen?" ... Being related to the Queen will not help them and nor will the fact that they spend holidays in magnificent royal castles assist them to get on in life. My wife and I have done our best to make our children recognize that the royal way of life they experience now and then is something to enjoy and appreciate but that it will never be a permanent part of their future lives.'

Sadly, another remark of Sir Angus's is especially poignant in retrospect. Speaking of the many occasions they had to put royal duties before their children he said: 'I think the time is coming very shortly when, if we don't see more of our children, we are going to pay the price at the other end when they're older.' He and Princess Alexandra had difficulties with their rebellious daughter Marina who had a public row with her parents over her baby and the boyfriend who later became her husband.

George St Andrews reacted quite differently when he fell in love with Sylvana Tomaselli, a graduate he met at Cambridge. From the first he must have known it was not going to be easy.

142

She was not only a Roman Catholic but had divorced her first husband. It was enough to send shock waves through the family but gentle, resolute George proved determined in his love for the dark-haired young woman from a very different background to his own. Sylvana was a research fellow in history, four years older; a thoughtful, clever girl who was at first wary of another close relationship after the failure of her first. George found she was a deeply serious person with a leaning towards meaningful, intellectual conversations which initially attracted him. They both found the long discussions intensely stimulating and before long the mutual interest had flared into a serious love affair. It seemed entirely natural to move in together into a small, terraced house George had bought in Cambridge.

When news of the liaison percolated through to York House, George's parents were quite naturally perturbed; when they realized the couple had resolved to marry they may well have remembered how long they themselves had to wait because of Princess Marina's opposition. They considered the implications and the likelihood of formidable disapproval from the Queen, appreciating that the proposed marriage would have been unthinkable even a generation ago when the Royal Family was still collectively bruised by the trauma of the Abdication. But the Queen's attitude to divorce has grown remarkably flexible over the years as social attitudes have changed and members of her own family have suffered the anguish and failure of broken marriages. The Kents had been through a similar scenario with Eddie's younger brother Michael when he married Marie Christine von Reibnitz, a Roman Catholic whose marriage had been annulled. Now they had to face up to George's steadfast insistence that Sylvana was the one woman for him.

He had always been the clever one of the Royal Family's 'Sixties' generation. 'Brainbox' his less gifted cousins called him when he won a King's scholarship to Eton where his father and uncle had been educated. But worry about his mother's illness had affected the sensitive teenager who was so close to her and he failed two of his three A-level exams. As the Duchess's condition improved, so did George's application to his school work and he eventually passed with top grades in history, English and French. He could be destined for a brilliant academic career counselled his headmaster. George, however, had shown previously that, in exams, his work could fluctuate. In 1984 he failed his history tripos (Part 1) at Cambridge where he had followed his elder cousin Prince Charles. But he persevered to graduate with a degree in history.

He was a quiet, retiring boy but beneath the surface possessed a strong will when his mind was made up, as his parents found when he told them he wished to marry Sylvana. Patiently, doggedly, George won his mother and father over to the marriage. Had he been a less mature and determined character they might have advised postponement for some years until he could support a wife. But, as he and Sylvana were already living together in such mutual concord, it seemed an unrealistic proposal.

Their minds must have harked back also to the four long years they themselves had waited to consolidate a relationship that has proved so stable throughout their thirty years of marriage – in sickness and in health. And, as one of the relatives pointed out: 'George needs someone whose intellectual capacity equals or exceeds his own. She is also rather beautiful which is a considerable bonus.'

As he was marrying a divorced Roman Catholic, George renounced his right of succession which could, however, pass to his children provided they were not brought up as Roman Catholics. The Queen, also, had to give her permission – necessary under the Royal Marriages Act – and, that done, the engagement was announced on 10 June 1987, the birthday of George's godfather, the Duke of Edinburgh.

His mother laid on a family celebration lunch at York House and the couple were photographed in the grounds of St James's Palace with Sylvana happily showing off her sapphire and diamond engagement ring which closely resembled the ring George's grandfather had given to his grandmother Marina. He had never liked formal parties and knowing this, Kate arranged another, very informal get-together in the grounds of Sandringham where the Royal Family had gathered for a New Year break. She worked out when there was a likelihood of a full moon and borrowed the Queen's log cabin, the scene of many a happy family celebration. Eating charcoal-grilled steaks in the moonlight with heat from a huge bonfire was a splendidly relaxed way to introduce Sylvana into a family circle she had hitherto only glimpsed on television or in newspaper photographs. But it was typical of the Duchess's thoughtfulness to give them exactly the sort of party they liked. She realized, perhaps, that Sylvana was naturally rather apprehensive of meeting such formidable in-laws en masse but that night she was 'positively glowing and obviously very much in love', said a Kent family friend.

Because of the Royal Marriage Act the couple were not allowed to marry in church or in a registry office in England or Wales. So they picked Leith Town Hall, Edinburgh, which was convenient as the Queen invited the Kent family to stay at Holyrood House, also used for the wedding reception.

It was a kindly gesture made despite the fact that, as Head of the Church, she could not herself attend the wedding; nor, for the same reason, could the Duke of Edinburgh and the Prince of Wales. But Princess Anne was there and all the Kent family to see the couple exchange their civil vows on a misty, cold January day in the austere surroundings of the Town Hall. As was not unnatural Kate and Eddie resolutely tried not to compare it with their own wedding in the splendid, rose-filled Minster. But they were heartened to see how contented and happy were George and Sylvana and that, as everyone present agreed, was a good omen for the future.

Soon after the wedding the young couple packed their belongings which included, as might be expected, masses of books, into George's Ford Escort and set off through Europe to Hungary which, at that time, was still behind the 'Iron Curtain'.

George was taking up a six months posting as Third Secretary in the Budapest Embassy to see if a working life in the Diplomatic Service would prove a fulfilling and useful career and whether he himself was suitable for it. Sylvana who had already published, as co-editor, a collection of essays on rape was working on another book about the Enlightenment – 'more particularly the Scottish and French Enlightenment', as she told me. This study of an eighteenth-century philosophical movement demanded lengthy research and kept her busy during the stay in Hungary and through her pregnancy.

They loved Budapest and Katharine, hearing the news of an expected grandchild, privately visited them there. They showed her the city they had come to love – the homeland of Liszt, Lehar and Bartok and George was reminded that his great-grandmother Queen Mary was descended from the Hungarian Countess Claudine Rhedy who was morganatically married to the royal Duke Alexander of Wurttemberg. Their son, Francis, Duke of Teck, was Queen Mary's father.

George and Sylvana came back to England in time for the birth of their baby son and to spend Christmas with the family at Anmer Hall from where they all went to Sandringham to join the Queen's luncheon party on Christmas Day. Afterwards they settled into the small terraced house in Cambridge where George prepared for his Foreign Office exams. Unfortunately and perhaps not entirely unexpectedly in view of his past record with exams he was expected to pass first time, he failed to pass the necessary standard. Perhaps the new baby proved too diverting for his concentration but it was a crushing disappointment which left Sylvana the only breadwinner for the time being.

In their thoroughly modern marriage, the couple are sharing the job of bringing up baby. When Sylvana goes out to her university work, George is left in charge – and vice versa. But when they spend weekends and holiday breaks with the family the Duchess employs a nanny to give them a break from baby-watching – although there is nothing she likes better than looking after her grandson herself. As Sarah Partridge puts it: 'The Duchess is basically a family lady.'

Helen, now promoted to 'Aunt', is a more extrovert character than her brother George and, for a time, her exuberance and the relative freedom she enjoyed post-school worried her parents who were never sure what she would be up to next. A steadying influence was her friendship with her cousin, Lady Sarah Armstrong-Jones, daughter of Princess Margaret and Lord Snowdon, who was born only two days after Helen and has been close to her ever since. The girls have inherited the artistic flair of both sets of parents and grandparents and their adult lives have been linked by similar occupations.

Sarah is an artist and Helen works for a fine art gallery. When they were growing up they formed a tightly-knit quartet with the other royals born in the 'baby-boom' of 1964. All but James Ogilvy, who works in the City, have followed artistic pursuits. Prince Edward works in Soho, not far from Sarah at the Royal Academy and Helen in Mayfair and they still meet frequently when Edward can tear himself away from theatre-land and his job with the theatre management company he joined after an initial grounding with Andrew Lloyd-Webber's Really Useful Theatre Company.

Helen is currently a director of the Karsten Schubert modern art gallery and this absorbing career fulfils the love she has for antiques and fine art inherited from both her paternal grand-parents, George and Marina and her great-grandmother Queen Mary. The Consort of George V was a great royal collector and her free time was invariably spent hunting for treasures in antique shops and galleries, often with Helen's grandfather, Prince George.

He was keenly interested in art and his collection became a notable one. Unfortunately most of it had to be reluctantly sold by his widow because she needed money after his death. Princess Marina's side of the family was also artistic. Her father, Prince Nicholas, was a talented artist and he sold work to help bring up his family and aid refugee charities when they were in exile in Paris. Two of his paintings are hung at Windsor Castle and others are in the homes of the Duke of Kent, Princess Alexandra and Prince Michael. Like her grandmother, Helen studied art in Paris after finishing her sixth-form year at Gordonstoun, the spartan school in Scotland where the Queen's three sons were educated.

Helen is an attractive blonde with her mother's sapphire eyes and much of the sparkle and vivacity of her grandfather, Prince George. Like him she broke some royal rules when she emerged into the adult world but her exploits were mostly very harmless and did no more than ruffle the feathers of some 'old guard' courtiers at Buckingham Palace.

She has much of the Duchess's generosity and kindness which was shown during her mother's illness when she was particularly sensitive and understanding. But it has taken her all her adult life – she is still only twenty-seven – to get used to publicity. She realizes now, and faces up to it wryly, that amongst royal women the media demand exceeds supply and so the younger fringe members still make good newsy stories.

As Helen's experience of the world grows so does her personal confidence. She no longer needs to be rebellious and her pro-motion to director of the firm she works for has been an added incentive to show a more settled face to the world. Like the Princess of Wales and the Duchess of York she adores London and the fashionable restaurants and night clubs. But, like her mother, she is a countrywoman also; migrating home for most weekends from her London flat.

She is the apple of her father's eye and knows how to handle him. They are very alike in temperament. Not the easiest man to live with, he cloaks what was once youthful high spirits with a dignified grouchiness these days and has a stubborn streak that has been inherited by his daughter.

Her first job was as a receptionist at Christie's, the auctioneers, where she was soon promoted to the Contemporary Art depart-ment. Then she went to New York to work for the company there, staying in their apartment in the Del Monico building which was, without doubt, a special perk for someone described as an ordinary employee. But in 'the Big Apple' Helen seemed 'a little subdued – probably because she is overwhelmed with all the new names and faces' said Roberta Maneker, Christie's spok-eswoman in the US. It was a comment her friends in Britain found hard to understand. 'It certainly doesn't sound like Melons,' said one of them, using the nickname bestowed on her at Gor-donstoun as a tribute to her shapely form.

She soon headed back to London; found a new job with Karsten Schubert, the fine art dealers, and a flat in Westminster which she shared with an old school friend Arabella Cobbold. She now lives in her own two-bedroomed flat in Earls Court. As often as possible she tries to share in the family breakfast at York House which the Duchess has described as the 'high spot' of her day. 'They know what I'm doing – I've tried very hard to involve them – and I hear what they're doing,' she said.

Helen has inherited her mother's fine dress sense – the Duchess has always been one of the most elegant of the royal women. Kate always goes to top couturiers for her working clothes but has been known to slip into Marks and Spencer for underwear. She loves bright, clear colours and simple but striking designs. Her clothes look comfortable but are always supremely well cut.

Princess Margaret, who does not dish out approval lightly, thinks very highly of Kate's clothes sense, once describing her as 'possibly the most stylish member of the Royal Family'. The Princess of Wales evidently thinks so too and followed the Duchess to the Emanuels – where she had been the first royal customer – for her wedding dress. 'We have been dressing the Duchess of Kent for ten years,' the husband and wife team said before their marriage and partnership split. 'Every royal tour and every Wimbledon and some of her classic white gowns for the Opening of Parliament.' Victor Edelstein is another designer, now a favourite of the Princess, where Kate had been a client for some years. According to the Emanuels (when they were together) the Duchess 'comes to our salon or we go to York House. We go through her itinerary and she tells us when she wants something special.'

One of the best photographs ever taken of the Duchess was by the late Norman Parkinson and in it she wore a filmy, ethereal white Emanuel creation which emphasized her air of luminous fragility. But she can look equally appealing, as she did when staying in Princess Margaret's villa on Mustique, windblown and carefree with a tropical flower tucked into her ponytail.

The Duchess's jewellery is magnificent although limited by royal standards. Some is part of the fabulous Romanov collection once worn by Tsarinas and Grand Duchesses. It was inherited from Princess Marina who, in turn, was left it by her mother

Princess Nicholas of Greece, an Imperial and Royal Highness and Grand Duchess of Russia. She began life as a princess of the Imperial court and ended it in a villa in Athens with a collection of stray cats which she had befriended.

Kate wears her jewellery with pride aware of the importance Princess Marina attached to family heirlooms. Unlike her sister-in-law Princess Michael who reportedly sold some fine jewellery and had them copied in paste, Kate wears only originals. But sometimes, off-duty, it is frankly fake-but-fun costume jewellery – the kind her daughter Helen adores.

Lord Nicholas Windsor, twenty-one in July, 1991, is the youngest of the Kent children and the one with whom Kate has spent most time.

Whilst George, his elder brother, takes after the Worsley family in looks, Nicholas is very like the Duke at the same age. He went to Westminster as a day pupil and not Eton like his father, brother and the Worsley uncles, because it was felt that having him return after school each afternoon would help his mother who, at that time, was in the throes of her depressive illness. He proved a happy and lively companion who excelled at tennis, a sport they all love.

Like his cousin James Ogilvy, he is enthusiastic about travel and a spell in East Africa with Operation Raleigh and four months in India and Nepal gave him a taste for more. So after a year at Manchester College, Oxford, studying philosophy, he planned a year's break to travel round the world 'broadening his experience'. Then he will continue his three-year course. The Duke and Duchess agreed to this plan after some deliberation. Nicholas has already caused concern because of an incident very close to home. He was cautioned by police in December 1988 after being found in the possession of a small amount of cannabis in St James's Park – a stone's throw from his home.

Although cannabis is a relatively harmless drug, it alarmed his parents and must have brought home to them that a royal youngster is as vulnerable, if not more so, as any other.

For the Duchess who has dealt with drug-users through her work with the Samaritans it would have been a particularly anxious time. But after a tough dressing-down from his father, a chastened Nicholas joined the Royal Family for Christmas a few days later, aware that, although little was said about his escapade, it had been front-page news. In view of the passionate interest his family, particularly the Queen and the Duke of Edinburgh, take in fighting drug abuse, his own minor episode had let the side down.

Hopefully it was an isolated incident, unlike his grandfather, the late Duke of Kent, who became an addict and was rescued from an increasingly downward path by his elder brother David, then Prince of Wales.

All in all this was an average pattern of family life in the last decade of the century but very different from that of Eddie and his sister Alex emerging into adulthood at the end of the Fifties. Their problem was convincing their mother they did not want to marry a Prince or Princess as she had planned for them.

In the next generation, George chose a Roman Catholic divorcee and Marina got pregnant without a wedding ring – an omission she later rectified but not without some harsh public words fired at her parents from the columns of a tabloid newspaper. For Eddie and Kate, both so close to the Ogilvys, it was a wretched time and they must have been thankful that, so far, the strong link they have with their own children has not been put to such a test.

151

14

No Fuss Please

Day by day the two worlds of the Duchess of Kent, the dignified, distant royal existence still hedged in with formality and outdated convention and the realms where 'protocol is thrown out of the window' which she encounters increasingly on her visits to hospices, hospitals and centres for the elderly, have grown closer together. In the process Katharine Kent is pioneering the kind of work the Princess of Wales is beginning to take on and finds so rewarding. Hopefully it may make the future Queen's life more personally fulfilling and less like the lament of Empress Eugenie of France who wrote to her sister: 'Destiny always has a sad side to it ... I who am always longing to be free have chained my life. I shall never be alone, never free. I shall be surrounded by the etiquette of the court whose principal victim I shall be.'

Her words may still be applicable to the more senior members of the Royal Family. But Kate has found an escape route from that 'gilded cage' which may have been one of the contributory factors in her breakdown and subsequent illness.

Once there would have been an unbreachable chasm between the attractive but somewhat aloof Duchess and the warmhearted woman who reaches out instinctively, these days, to touch and make contact with those people who have a real need to be cherished and comforted. Now it seems the façade of royalty has merged with that of the woman who admits she feels humble and privileged when she leaves a hospice. She gives as much time as she can, particularly to dying children, who themselves, unconsciously, give her the courage to continue her work. Suffering is relative and Kate finds the migraine that plagued her when she arrived on one of those visits vanished within a short time.

She wants no red carpets and formality and does not get it with those who know her well, such as Mother Frances Dominica at Helen House. 'I'd much rather people didn't take too much trouble,' she says. But, of course, they do go to great lengths on most official engagements to welcome a royal in the way that is considered appropriate however much better the money could be spent. 'We get so tired of the smell of fresh paint,' said the Princess of Wales once.

Down to earth as she is, the Duchess, although indoctrinated, as all the Family, with a belief in the conservation of the royal 'mystique', prefers not to be deferred to in too extreme a way. Inside the royal persona is a woman called Kate who finds the obsequiousness handed out to members of the Royal Family somewhat ambiguous in most of the places she finds herself, where comfort and reassurance count more highly than curtsies and red carpets.

Although she asks for no fuss she inevitably gets it which, although paradoxical, is balanced by the pleasure her royal presence brings. And if that means bowing and scraping – so be it. But it is a somewhat wry acceptance of pomp and ceremony by this straightforward royal who stands in a queue at a supermarket pay-out and slips up to a West End 'Kentucky Chicken' for the family supper.

Unlike the younger royal princesses, Katharine does not receive blanket media exposure as she goes about her work. She laughs about what she calls her claim to worldwide fame: the yearly tennis championships in London.

Once on an official visit to a remote part of India she heard someone say: 'There's that lady from Wimbledon.' And it is the same all over the world.

Like all the Kents, the Duchess loves tennis and has made several friends amongst world-class players. She enjoys a good football match, is a keen Liverpool supporter and was delighted when her husband became President of the FA, ensuring a prime seat at the Cup Final.

Brought up in a famous Yorkshire cricketing family, she watches play whenever she can. But opening the new Headingly nets she found she had forgotten her father's early teaching. A young schoolboy asked her to bowl a ball at him. Being Willy Worsley's daughter she could not resist but found she had lost the art. 'First thing I did I hit a photographer's camera – hard!' Then, a few moments later, she hit the same man on the elbow. 'A bit of a tricky time', she described the incident later.

The Duchess is 'very heavily musically orientated' as Sarah Partridge described her involvement with the many musical organizations amongst her list of patronages. Indeed, music is a very important part of her life as it is for her husband. It forms a bond between them which has seen them through some testing personal trials.

Whether it is singing nursery rhymes to the sick children at Helen House or as one of the sopranos in the chorus of the world-renowned Bach Choir, Kate's life is orchestrated to a great extent by music.

It is in her Worsley blood, nurtured by the family who gave Yorkshire the Hovingham Music Festivals to which great performers travelled considerable distances to appear in the improvised auditorium, in Thomas the Builder's Riding School.

The Duchess, now an accomplished pianist, had her first lessons from a teacher who came to Hovingham twice a week from nearby Malton. As a teenager she wanted to be a musician and, in choosing Runton, her parents found a school that encouraged musical talent with lessons in piano, clarinet, violin, oboe, bassoon and flute.

During her stay in Oxford, Kate had more advanced music lessons and felt qualified to take over some of the organization for the revival of the Festival when she returned home. Training the village children to sing grand opera was quite a feat and another was the discovery – whilst searching for music stands in the attics – of an ancient and valuable harpsichord. Restored and reconditioned it is now one of the many treasures of Hovingham Hall.

Anticipating future years when she would be a member of the Bach Choir, Katharine first sang in chorus at one of the Festivals when Marina de Gabarain, the Italian singer, came from Glyndebourne. She also played the organ regularly in Hovingham Church and still loves organ music following the royal tradition of Henry VIII who was a player of considerable skill, as was Prince Albert, Consort of Queen Victoria.

But it has been her singing with the Bach Choir which has not only been a considerable achievement personally, but also a safety-valve after her emergence from illness; altogether, a 'very important part of her life', according to lady-in-waiting Sarah Partridge.

In 1978, when she first joined the distinguished choir, her inclusion was no royal sinecure. Each of the 300 members, all amateurs, have a stiff audition followed by a re-audition every three years. No exception was made for the Duchess who had to be up to the standard demanded or it would affect the performance of the whole choir.

She attends most rehearsals, has developed friends in the choir and usually comes to their get-togethers and parties. All the members contribute something on these occasions, says spokeswoman Marian Needham and the Duchess never forgets to bring a contribution. Once she turned up carrying a tray of jam tarts she'd baked herself. It was clearly a happier appearance than when she was given permission by doctors to slip out of King Edward VII Hospital to sing as much-needed therapy in the bad days of her illness.

Formed in 1875, the Choir has always had royal associations. Queen Victoria became its first patron in 1879 and one of her daughters, Princess Christian, sang as a choir member. The Queen, as Princess Elizabeth, became patron in 1947 and in the centenary year the Prince of Wales became President.

He takes a great interest, has sung on several occasions in public concerts and insisted the Choir sing at his wedding in St Paul's Cathedral on 19 July 1981.

They give seven concerts a year in London in which the

Duchess nearly always sings. Included are performances of Bach's St Matthew Passion on the two Sundays before Easter in the Royal Festival Hall and two family carol concerts in the Royal Albert Hall. In addition there are concerts in places like King's College Chapel, Cambridge, St George's Chapel in Windsor Castle and occasional private performances in the Castle for the Queen and other members of the Royal Family.

Overseas tours have included Italy, Portugal, Holland, France, Germany, Hong Kong, Jerusalem and Norway and the 'magnificent, full-blooded singing', as a critic described it, has been helped by the fine soprano of Kate Kent, a performer in 'the choir which has developed into one of the finest in Europe', as another critic wrote.

The Duchess has made several memorable friends in the world of music among them the late Jacqueline du Pré with whom she was very close until her death. Sir Yehudi Menuhin is another world figure in music with whom the Kents are friendly and the Duchess is Patron of the school he has set up to train young musicians. Another patronage is the BBC's Young Musician of the Year, a competition she very much enjoys and encourages. She is also Joint-Patron, with the Duke, of the Hungarian Festival and was guest of honour at a Britain Salutes Hungary gala concert. It was of especial interest because of the Duke's Hungarian ancestry, through his grandmother Queen Mary, and their son and daughter-in-law's stay in Budapest when Lord St Andrews was attached to the British Embassy.

Eddie and Kate listened entranced to the sinuous, Slavonic music of Kodaly, the fine compelling Concerto for Orchestra by Bartok and the Piano Concerto No 1 by Liszt, which brought back happy memories of Budapest when George and Sylvana showed them around.

The Duchess's musical interests range wide. She will always be personally involved, if it is possible, in the Hong Kong Academy for the Performing Arts of which she is patron, however the future of the colony and its organizations change after the hand-over to China.

The Queensland Conservatorium of Music is another patronage whose progress she follows and visits whenever an Australian tour makes it possible. To the Ulster College of Music she makes regular visits in a surveillance-conscious area where royals are treated as high security risks because of IRA threats.

On one such visit the Duchess's helicopter was forced to land and she continued her journey by armoured car – a procedure usually regarded as too dangerous for members of the Royal Family visiting Northern Ireland.

Other musical organizations close to the Duchess's heart are the Royal Northern College of Music, the Northern Sinfonia Orchestra, the York Festival and mystery plays and the Leeds International Pianoforte Competition, all adjacent to her Yorkshire roots.

The Norfolk and Norwich Triennial Festival of Music and Arts is another of her organizations near her old home at Anmer Hall and the Newbury Spring Festival is not too far from her new home near Henley.

But in the interests of music Kate will travel far and wide. Like the Queen Mother, she flies frequently by helicopter enjoying and echoing 'Aunt Elizabeth's' family joke that 'the chopper has transformed my life as it did that of Anne Boleyn'.

15

A Light Shining

A royal in the Nineties has no real power but can still have enormous influence on the national awareness. But sometimes the media hype disturbs the Queen and her advisers who fear it could just as easily swing the other way, as indeed it has done in the past.

In a lecture Sir William Heseltine, formerly the Queen's forward-thinking Private Secretary, made some little-reported but pertinent remarks on the whole problem. 'Are they [the Royal Family] themselves to blame in some degree by admitting the TV cameras to their private lives for the making of the Royal Family film?' he wondered. 'The argument then was that the family appeared in the press as unreal cardboard figures – no happy mean between the court circular with its quaint archaisms and the messiness of the gossip columns.'

In keeping a low private profile and determinedly blocking any intrusion into their personal lives, Eddie and Kate work quietly on with little publicity and absolutely no razzamatazz.

But the hours they clock in, measured in the Duchess's case by her small staff's watchfulness about her health, are still impressive added to their behind-the-scenes work for varied causes. There is mounting appreciation particularly of the Duchess's projects and she is becoming increasingly loved and respected even though the younger royal women capture all the publicity. 'Nobody knows how much she does because she doesn't travel with hordes of reporters and photographers,' said the spokeswoman of one of her charities.

The Queen is very fond of these Kent cousins and leans on Eddie for his experience of ceremonial functions which he always does impeccably if a little woodenly.

This public image belies the man beneath who 'might look a bit glum but he's a great guy', according to one New Zealand civil servant who found himself sitting at dinner with the Kents somewhere in the back-of-beyond on a royal tour. Earlier a telephone call had invited him 'to dinner with Kathy and Ted' which turned out to be a very relaxed affair.

The Duchess's lady-in-waiting Carola Godman Irvine, carefree after the formalities of the day, was laughing about Kate's dignified aura when visiting the evil-smelling Rotorua Springs. It could have been because the awful aroma made her want to giggle but 'you looked just like Queen Victoria', joked Carola.

'Kathy', said the civil servant, 'had been playing with a bowl of chocolate mints and as the lady-in-waiting went on teasing she picked up a handful and threw them at her across the table.' The gales of laughter and applause were led by her husband.

Her own puckish sense of humour perks up her public appearances. At a Cancer Appeal Macmillan Fund rest centre a woman she met mentioned her small dog needed exercising. 'I knew there was a good reason I came here today,' joked the Duchess and took the dog 'walkies' on a lead for the rest of the engagement.

Now that she is back on form after her illness she and her husband are forging even stronger bonds as they celebrate thirty years of marriage. There has always been deep love and affection between them – 'and in addition they make each other laugh', commented a friend.

But it does not take much knowledge of human nature to know that it cannot always have been easy. German, Scandinavian, Russian and Hungarian blended with his British ancestry have produced a man well able to relax with his family and close friends but who tends to be 'rather grand' with lesser mortals as someone on the receiving end of his aloof disdain put it. Strong influences in his life were Queen Mary with whom he and his sister spent the war years and his mother, Princess Marina, both *grande dames* of the old school of royalty. Eddie takes after his great-grandfather and uncle inheriting the famous Windsor temper and can have an exceedingly short fuse on occasions.

He is immensely protective of his wife and proud of the effective work with which she is filling her life although sometimes he gets irritated if she is not around when he is at home. It doesn't often happen as he is as busy as she is but, like her, his activities seldom get any column inches apart from the court circular.

He pulls his full weight as a member of the Queen's team and has acted as a Counsellor of State during the Sovereign's absence abroad. He is an Honorary Freeman and Liveryman of the Worshipful Company of Clothworkers and the Worshipful Company of Salters; he followed family tradition by becoming a Freemason and was elected Grand Master of the United Grand Lodge of England in 1967. He is a Grand Master of the Order of St Michael and St George and was made a Knight of the Garter in 1985.

He is also Personal Aide-de-Camp to the Queen, Colonel of the Scots Guards, Colonel-in-Chief of the Royal Regiment of Fusiliers, of the Devonshire and Dorset Regiment and of the Lorne Scots Regiment (in Canada). He is President of the Royal Institution, the Royal National Lifeboat Institution and the Royal United Services Institute for Defence Studies.

Other appointments are Chancellor of Surrey University, Chairman of the National Electronics Council and a past President of the Institute of Electrical and Radio Engineers. In addition there is his job with the British Overseas Trade Board as an ambassador for the nation's exports.

For this he receives a salary which helps ease the financial problems which have plagued him all his adult life. His Civil List allowance comes out of the Queen's own income and it would embarrass him to ask for more. A considerable amount of the expenses he and Katharine incurred in royal duties were subsidized by themselves – a situation the Queen eased by granting them a grace-and-favour residence at York House and the use of Anmer Hall on the Sandringham estate, the Queen's own private property.

Two more directorships – with British Insulated Callenders Cables PLC and Vickers PLC – have made the Kents more financially comfortable and able to afford their new home in Oxfordshire.

The advent of Sylvana, their new daughter-in-law, who supervises history and politics students at Cambridge and is dark, intense and intellectual, into the home circle has widened their horizons still further.

Katharine's ability to make her new daughter-in-law feel part of the family has resulted in a mutually rewarding understanding between the two women from very different backgrounds. The younger couple and their son regularly weekend and holiday with Kate and Eddie in their home near Henley-on-Thames which so closely resembles the much-loved Coppins.

Croker End House, bought from their friends the Earl and Countess of Arran, is a former vicarage in Nettlebed, Oxfordshire and is the first house they have owned since they sold Coppins. 'It is a marvellous family home,' said Lord Campbell of Eskan who once lived there, 'it has an enchanting atmosphere.'

Neighbours, including former Beatle George Harrison, are delighted the Kents have bought the house according to local barman Shaun Gilmore at the White Hart, because 'they are so unstuffy'.

But the royal presence posed some problems for the local police. One of the reasons they sold Coppins was security and the same headaches have arisen with their new home. Royal Protection officers led by the Chief Constable of Thames Valley police, Colin Smith, were disturbed at the difficulty of guarding Croker End House and the immediate proximity of a footpath. The Chief Constable, only too aware of the difficulties after supervising a security review at Buckingham Palace after Michael Fagan was found in the Queen's bedroom in 1982, felt the house was very vulnerable.

Modern royalty is perpetually heavily guarded. Most of them figure in terrorist hit lists and Royal Protection Squad officers undergo special training with the SAS. They study bomb security measures and are taught to use the most up-to-date German-made

Heckler and Koch sub-machine gun which fires fifteen bullets in a second, weighs only four pounds, is thirteen inches long and can be carried in a holster and fired from the hip.

New terrorist threats add to the stress of members of the Royal Family who have a demanding job to do under ordinary conditions. For a normal engagement visiting a school in Lingfield, Surrey, Katharine was guarded by dozens of armed police officers who had been on duty since dawn combing the grounds with tracker dogs.

'One has to be permanently alert whilst trying not to think about it,' a lady-in-waiting told me. 'Really it is just a fact of life we have to face.'

That is why it is so necessary to have a peaceful haven for weekends and holidays where, in the Duchess's case, she can spend therapeutic hours in the garden, as her mother used to do at Hovingham Hall, with the small Kate pottering behind with her watering can and spade. 'Relaxed, her public reticence vanishes and she appears a natural, happy woman with an almost childlike eagerness to get to know a person better,' said an acquaintance who soon became a friend. 'Looking at her now it is difficult to believe that someone so calm and serene could have been so tormented.'

Her homes have that beeswax and lemony smell that speaks of old furniture carefully polished. Splashes of colour light up the rooms where flowers have been arranged, not too stiffly, but with natural flair. There are oil paintings of Eddie's royal ancestors and masses of family photographs of Windsors and Worsleys.

She travels to her engagements in an ancient Rolls which once belonged to Princess Marina. It is not entirely reliable and once broke down outside a London hospital where the Duchess was opening a new department. 'It's always doing that. We'll call the AA,' said her detective resignedly.

The classic black limousine has a perennial reminder of George and Marina: a silver St Christopher set behind delicate silver gates in the partition between the front and back seats.

Once, leaving the Royal Opera House, a man darted from the crowd and tried to get into the car. With evident faith in her

talisman Kate told restraining police officers: 'Please let him go –
he only wants to talk to me.'

But she is not always chauffeur-driven and often travels by
London taxi. One London cabbie picked up the Duchess for the
second time and when she recognized him, in one of her charming
spontaneous gestures, she gave him a yellow rose from the bunch
she was carrying.

'My wife will never believe you've been in my cab – she didn't
the last time,' said the cabbie. 'She'll say I bought the rose at a
florist.' So the Duchess wrote on a visiting card: 'To Valerie with
very best wishes from Katharine'.

It is this ability to shift gear from royalty on parade to ordinary
woman in the street that so charms those whose lives touch that
of the Duchess, however briefly. She genuinely likes people 'to
be themselves' and was delighted when a teenage cellist at the
Young Musician of the Year competition candidly told her his
favourite things were 'his girlfriend, eating chocolate and watching "Neighbours" on television'.

Kate follows the politician's ploy of kissing babies but she does
it straight from the heart because she wants to make contact with
another tiny human being. 'Hello my little precious' she'll say,
hugging a frail bundle at a hospice.

She has never had a hard time from the press despite over-
protective staff who try to maintain a distance from the media
and can be frustrating in their efforts to keep their friendly
Duchess aloof.

John Junor, newspaper columnist of the *Mail on Sunday*, often
a stern critic of the Royal Family, admires her greatly. He
described the Duchess as having 'a rare quality that shines from
her face. A quality of compassion for the suffering of others'.

Another columnist who can also be abrasive about the royals
when she deems it necessary, Jean Rook of the *Daily Express*,
positively rhapsodized in a piece headed 'The caring that crowns
a Duchess'. Of Kate's appearance one night on television she
wrote: 'Her light brightened millions with heavy hearts this week
when they saw her cradling a dying baby. As if she were trying
to hold the entire wretched world in her arms ... this once shy

Yorkshire lass is one of us. One of the best of us.'

To the public she is not very well known, although mention of her name always evokes a smile and most women remember her spell of illness with which, to some degree, they can identify and sympathize with, whilst admiring the way in which she rallied and came back into public life.

Speaking at a Woman of the Year luncheon in London on the theme 'Give me time', the Duchess almost moved the audience of distinguished women to tears as she spoke of her work with children and the elderly and praised many young helpers who give their time to the caring organizations.

'We may not have long but we can live each moment intensely,' she said. 'We have no excuse for being bored.'

It is an inspirational note the Duchess takes with her into the future; a metaphorical light shining, like her smile, on the years ahead.

AUTHOR'S NOTE

When I started researching the Duchess's story there was one area of her life about which I felt uncertain how to proceed: the depressive illness which marred her late forties and early fifties and was so worrying for her family.

But I met a wise, compassionate and very senior person among the medical staff gathered at a hospital to greet the Duchess. 'I do hope you are going to mention that unhappy, traumatic time because it has shaped her life ever since and is important to her story' I was told.

That is my reason for writing about this deeply personal area of the Duchess's life. As I am not – and would not wish to be – privy to the full details of her illness, I have mentioned only the facts which are common to many such cases where bereavement of whatever kind produces such severe depression that it results in hospitalization. I hope the Duchess's courageous recovery and her subsequent dedication to the suffering and despair of others may prove an inspiration to anyone who has to endure the same experience.

Valerie Garner

BIBLIOGRAPHY

AIRLIE, Mabell, Countess of, *Thatched with Gold*, Hutchinson 1962

BUCKLE, Richard (Ed), *Self-Portrait with Friends: The Selected Diaries of Cecil Beaton*, Weidenfeld and Nicholson 1979

COWARD, Noel, *Diaries* edited by Grahame Payne and Sheridan Morley, Weidenfeld and Nicolson 1982

CATHCART, Helen, *The Duchess of Kent*, W.H. Allen 1971

CHANNON, Henry, Sir (Chips), *Diaries* edited by Robert Rhodes Graves Weidenfeld and Nicolson 1967

CHRISTOPHER, Prince of Greece, *Memoirs*, Hurst and Blackett 1938

FIELD, Leslie, *The Queen's Jewels*, Weidenfeld and Nicolson 1987

GARNER, Valerie, *My Young Friends*, Weidenfeld and Nicolson 1989

GARNER, Valerie, *Debretts Tribute to Queen Elizabeth the Queen Mother*, Webb and Bower 1990

MORROW, Ann, *The Queen*, Granada 1983

NICHOLAS, Prince of Greece, *My Fifty Years*, Hutchinson 1926

POPE-HENNESSEY, James, *Queen Mary*, George Allen and Unwin 1959

VICKERS, Hugo, *Cecil Beaton*, Weidenfeld and Nicolson 1985

WARWICK, Christopher, *George and Marina*, Weidenfeld and Nicolson 1988

WARWICK, Christopher, *Two Centuries of Royal Weddings*, Dodd Mead 1980

WENTWORTH-DAY, James, *HRH Princess Marina of Kent*, Robert Hale 1962

WHITING, Audrey, *The Kents*, Futura 1985

WINDSOR, Duchess of, *The Heart Has Its Reasons*, Michael Joseph 1956

INDEX

In this index 'Eddie' = Edward George, Duke of Kent, and 'Kate' = Katharine, Duchess of Kent